CREATIVE
FOOD
PHOTOGRAPHY

CREATIVE FOOD PHOTOGRAPHY

HOW TO
CAPTURE
EXCEPTIONAL
IMAGES
OF FOOD

KIMBERLY ESPINEL

contents

introduction

Food is a love story and growing up in a home where food was at the centre of *everything*, it's one I know all too well...

But while my love of food was inevitable, my love of food photography was a big, crazy and rather wonderful accident. Back in 2013, I was an adoption social worker, living the 9-to-5 and desperately trying to juggle my career with motherhood. Although I felt I was in a meaningful profession, something was missing.

I'd never owned a camera before, yet I still vividly remember reading food blogs for the very first time that year and knowing, instantly, that I wanted in. Just the thought of sharing my passion for plant-based foods with the wider world got me excited, and the possibility of the recipes I had carefully crafted finding a place in someone else's kitchen gave me the hope that I could contribute to a bigger purpose. All that, coupled with the spontaneous decision to purchase a second-hand camera on eBay, led to the start of my tumultuous love affair with food photography.

At first, as I tried to capture the food images I wanted, I failed many times (more than I care to remember), but I always stopped short of giving up. Despite the tears and seemingly endless disappointments, providing my creativity with an outlet felt incredibly invigorating. So much so, that my obsession with food photography soon overtook my obsession with writing recipes by a long stretch.

I saw food photography as an opportunity to celebrate the foods that come from the soil and share my enthusiasm for eating plants with the wider world. Unsurprisingly, my food stories (including the ones in this book!) always involve plants on plates, be they fruits, vegetables, herbs, legumes or grains: any seasonal, plant-based foods I can get my hands on, shown off in the best possible light, so that no one can ever deny that eating plants is pretty darn sexy!

Food photography is powerful. I have seen it work its magic not just on me, but on the thousands of creatives to whom I have had the honour of teaching this delicious art form. It's so powerful, in fact , that it completely changed the trajectory of my life. In the summer of 2016, I made the life-changing decision to quit my 15 year-long career as a social worker and dedicate every working hour to food photography. It remains, hands down, one of the best choices I've ever made.

My guess is, if you picked up this book, you're as enamoured with food photography as I am. Maybe you're hoping to write and photograph your own cookbook, or like me, make the transition into a fulfilling and creative profession. Maybe you just long to fine-tune your food images for the sheer joy of it. Maybe you turned to this book because you're looking for inspiration to help you find your own style and finally feel ready to take the kind of food photos you've dreamed of for so long. If any of these options sounds like you, you've come to the right place.

This book is for creatives who want to know what it really takes to become a food photographer with a signature look, what it takes to approach your photography with intention and clarity, and how to hone your craft beyond the boundaries of your imagination. This book is for those who want to shoot images that stand out, evoke emotion and tell a delicious and beautiful food story. This book is for anyone seeking to go deeper and inch closer to their creative potential with curiosity, heart and an insatiable desire to share their love of food and photography with the world.

This book doesn't offer a one-size-fits-all, cookie-cutter approach to food photography and food styling. It doesn't contain technical photography information that you could easily Google or find on YouTube. It's also not a book aimed at the complete beginner who has never taken a food image before and isn't sure if food photography is worth all the fuss. It's not a 'do-A-so-you-get-to-B' prescriptive manual (who wants to stop at B, anyway?) and it doesn't provide linear answers or too-good-to-be true short cuts to a lucrative career in food photography. If that's what you're after, this book isn't for you.

This book *does* give you permission to go on a journey to find out what it is about food and photography that makes your heart beat faster: what defines your unique style and how to translate that into a food image you're truly proud of. It's about using intention, exploration, creativity, play and purpose to tell your food story in the way that is right for you.

Gaining the confidence to consistently deliver stand-out images depends as much on capturing them as it does on your ability to plan a photo shoot down to a T. The ability to plan like a pro is a vital skill you need to develop if you're hoping to work as part of a professional team, to create for a client or to shoot a cookbook. Even if you're capturing food for your eyes only, entering a shoot with focus and a clear end goal in mind (as well as a road map for how to get there) is everything.

This book shares with you the tried-and-tested processes you need to plan your shoot with care, empowering you to capture food images that say more than a thousand words. This book will help you to develop a deep understanding of colour theory and consequently be bolder in your approach to colours than ever before. This book is here to fuel your courage to play with light and shadow, to look at them with fresh eyes, and make powerful, thoughtful decisions when it comes to working with your camera. This book also contains *lots* of ideas on how to approach your composition so that it feels dynamic, fun and always interesting.

Outstanding food photography and food styling is as much about knowing the technical aspects as it is about being creative, playful and heartfelt. Where other food photography books and online resources focus predominantly on the former, this book is about diving deep into the latter, because *that's* what will set you apart and enable you to capture truly noteworthy images. This book is here to gently nudge you along your path as you explore how to get the finer details of a food image spot on. Food styling, image editing, backdrop selection, the curation of the loveliest prop collection – everything matters, which is why this book covers it all.

It takes courage to create food images that are authentic and beautiful. Years of teaching food photography and food styling have taught me that the more vulnerable and courageous you are in sharing food images with soul, the more rewarding the process. More learning opportunities arise, and you make more progress. I have seen evidence of this time and again, particularly during my #eatcaptureshare Instagram food photography challenge, a four-week online challenge that attracts thousands of food lovers from around the world and invites them to create and share images based around different weekly themes. It is always the people who dare to try and fail and stand up and try again, those who share their authentic selves, who rise to the top and create images that win over everyone's heart.

More than a simple food photography and food styling book, *Creative Food Photography* is a heartfelt, thorough guide on how to live your best creative life as a food lover and food photographer. It came to be because, as I said, food is a love story, and I fundamentally believe that every love story deserves to be told. Your camera is the best tool I can think of for you to share your food story with the world. So, pick up your camera, grab something delicious to eat and let's get stuck in, shall we?

Kimberly Espinel

part one

PLANNING

one

FINDING YOUR STYLE

finding your style

The world needs *you*! Yes, that's right, you: *your* food, *your* vision, *your* creativity. Think about it: there are billions of people walking the surface of this earth, yet none of them see the world the way you do, none of them have the exact innate creative powers that you have, and consequently none of them can capture food through their lens the way I know you can.

As a food photographer, *who you are* and *how you see the world* will naturally spill over into what you create with your camera.

I believe that success and fulfilment in this field lie in your capacity to walk your own path and create food stories that no one else can tell like you can.

You're your own unique being: your own quirky self with boundless innate creative potential. So, let's unravel that creative vision.

Perhaps, like me, your food photography and food styling journey started by accident and you just can't shake off the feeling that you're an imposter, that you're just pretending to be a photographer, chef or food stylist and that any minute now, someone will ask you for your qualifications and you'll want the ground to swallow you up, 'cos you haven't got any! I get it; I've been there.

Manifesting your innate creative power can be scary and vulnerable. That's why it's often easier to just blend in, follow suit and get distracted by what other people are doing. In the world of food photography and styling, that might look like copying someone else's composition, using the same baking recipe as the person you admire or following particular colour trends because they're so popular on social networking sites.

Although imitating and learning from others form important stepping stones on your creative journey, I believe you'll only really create beautiful, delicious and powerful images that you're truly proud of once you allow your own approach and style to guide your creative process.

If you create with your internal compass as a guide, you're more likely to get your work noticed, to grow a loyal audience whose hearts beat to the same drum as yours, and to make a living doing what you love. You'll find more joy in shooting and styling than ever before, because there is no better feeling than creating as your authentic self and making meaningful work that is different and uniquely yours. Moreover, you'll be fulfilling your creative purpose: the one that put you on this earth in the first place! In doing so, you'll avoid bottling up that creative energy and instead give your creativity the outlet it deserves and desperately craves. Creating what lights that fire in your belly will help you identify your special place in this crazy, busy world.

My mission with this book is to empower you to be your authentic, creative self and allow your individuality to shine through in your food styling and food photography. I've written this to give you the tools you need to tell *your* food story, one that people will want to engage with. Yes, there will be stumbling blocks along the way, but I'm here to guide you through those, and give you the strength you need to pick yourself up, dust yourself off and shoot those stunning food images you've always dreamed of capturing.

perfect imperfection

Just this week I was working on an assignment for a client and I had a junior assistant helping out in the studio. We were setting up a scene where nature's bounty was to be celebrated, and the carrots we were photographing still had some dirt on them. Some of that soil fell on to the food photography backdrop; my assistant, as yet unfamiliar with my method of styling, wiped all the soil away so that the scene would look perfectly pristine, but to her surprise I asked her to put all the soil back, exactly where she'd found it.

My assistant's approach wasn't unusual. Many of my students are eager to learn how to create natural and effortless-looking food images, but when I invite them to leave the crumbs they have accidentally made on the table or suggest they show dirty spoons on a plate, they get visibly uncomfortable. Why is that?

Splashes, drips, drizzles and crumbs are the stuff that give our images meaning and energy, yet the concept of perfectionism has really been drilled into us. Images of the homes, gardens, people and places that we celebrate usually meet our idealistic vision of what perfection should look like. Homes need to have beautifully painted front doors and symmetrical windows, gardens require perfectly cut hedges, people need to have immaculate skin free of blemishes and wrinkles, and places should be spotless with rows of buildings that have a similar aesthetic and architectural pedigree.

Images that are perfect, where everything is in a dedicated, set position can indeed look pretty; in fact, they can look stunning. Just think of those Michelin-starred restaurants where the chefs plate food so immaculately you're left in complete and utter awe. One of the reasons they win Michelin stars is because their food looks perfect, but they are the exception to the rule. Sometimes when we aim for perfection in our food photography, we run the risk of creating images that look sterile and completely soulless. Soulless images won't move people; soulless images don't sell.

When we steer our images towards perfection, we are often following rules and guidelines set around society's views of what perfection is rather than tuning into our own sense of style and beauty. The consequence is that we end up adhering to current trends and creating food images that look just like those shot by everyone else, because we are all chasing those very same imposed standards of idealism and perfection. In other words, aiming for perfection in our photography robs our images of their individuality.

Holding on to this concept of perfection can give us a sense of security, albeit temporary. It allows us to hide who we really are as creatives and food photographers; it makes us feel like part of the pack. As part of the pack, we are less likely to experience painful rejection. However, this fear of rejection, of doing things wrong and of making mistakes is holding us back from finding our authentic selves, our true style and unique approach. Playing safe makes it less likely that we'll capture something with our camera that'll truly make our heart (or the hearts of audience) sing.

So, I say, let's throw those ideas of perfection out of the window and embrace food as a reflection of life as it really is: messy, interesting and perfectly imperfect. I've since come to learn that there is a Japanese term for this approach, called *wabi-sabi*. The idea behind *wabi-sabi* is that there's beauty in imperfection. Rather than seek to erase or rectify imperfection, in life we should embrace crumbling walls, wildflowers, a crooked nose and the occasional graffiti here and there. In food styling, this could mean allowing a berry that's moved out of place or a drop of olive oil that's fallen by accident, to just *be*. Are you breaking out in a sweat just at the thought? If so, please listen up!

When you embrace imperfection in your food styling and composition, what you are actually doing is embracing your own imperfections and individuality. You're tapping into your unique superpower: being your own creative self, which no one else can be! I believe that when you do that, you break away from soulless images and move towards developing your own signature look and stand-out style.

In rejecting these broad perceptions of perfection and how things 'should' be, you are doing one more crucial thing. You are creating imagery that has the potential to evoke emotions in others. What you are doing is creating food images that feel real and relatable and beautiful, all at the same time. I mean, think about it: is your dining table at home free of crumbs, the occasional spilled coffee or sticky jam patches? No? I didn't think so!

Throughout this book you'll read about the importance of planning, being intentional, thinking through colours, textures and composition, and approaching the process of food photography thoughtfully. You might wonder whether the idea of *wabi-sabi* is contradictory to that strategic approach. I say, you do have to plan and be intentional in order to create truly stand-out images; however, I invite you to wholeheartedly embrace the opportunity to inject these images with your unique personality, perspective and imperfection – and see what happens.

I invite you to wholeheartedly embrace the opportunity to inject these images with your *unique personality, perspective* and *imperfection*.

the magical power of inspiration

Just like cooking a delicious and elaborate three-course meal, capturing beautiful food images requires creative energy from deep within us. The more we want to create, the more we need to have in our well of inspiration, in order to be able to draw from it.

Inspiration adds that spring to our step. Without inspiration, our work can become stagnant, homogeneous, lifeless and, worst of all, boring! Inspiration is the compost of creativity: the very soil in which the fruit of our labours is first cultivated.

True inspiration is magical. It can invigorate us and guide us towards finding our unique vision, voice and taste. It can spark an idea and provide a starting point for shooting that food story we've been thinking about for days. Fresh sources of inspiration help us flow through periods of creative stagnation and ensure we capture new and exciting food photos, ones that surprise and delight us and our clients, as well as our audience.

So, how can we replenish our creative well and ensure new-found creative energy supports us in finding our style rather than leading us astray? Inspiration is everywhere; finding the inspiration which nourishes our soul and lights the flame in our belly is our goal.

Venture into nature

The colours and textures I find in nature heavily influence my work, and I bet that Mother Nature can spark inspiration in your photography and styling too. If you're not sure where to start, how about going for a long walk in a local woodland, along a beautiful river or on a sandy beach? Observe and take note of the different colours you encounter on your stroll: can you incorporate the prettiest of these colour combinations into your food photography work? Why not visit your local farmer's market and take stock of what fruits, herbs and vegetables are in season in your area? Allow them to set the tone for the images you shoot that week. Or how about letting the energy of the sun inspire your work? I'm definitely a light chaser, and I am fascinated by how the sun affects light and shadow points as well as the temperature of my work. Exploring light and shadow is so important for us as food photographers that we'll study it in a lot more depth in **Finding Your Light** (page 69) and **Lighting Your Star** (page 104).

Become a renaissance man/woman

The artist Leonardo da Vinci was not only an incredible painter, but a sculptor, engineer *and* architect. The late Maya Angelou excelled as a writer, poet *and* public speaker. Tapping into their creativity (and genius!) in one area greatly helped them get inspired in other areas too. In the same way, pursuing an array of hobbies and interests has the potential to make you a better photographer. What will you choose to master next?

Eat at a new restaurant

Cooking brings so much joy, but eating out is extra special. It's also an opportunity to get lots of food photography inspiration. You get to taste new flavour combinations that can inform how you construct a dish you aim to photograph. You also get to closely study someone else's plating and food styling finishing touches, offering you lots of new ideas.

Lose yourself in a great book

Did you know that reading a book for 30 minutes a day makes you more creative? That's because it encourages you to think, to fantasise and to use your imagination. It also enables you to better concentrate and develop your problem-solving skills. Reading opens up new worlds and allows you to see things through a different lens. Whether it be a gripping novel, a thought-provoking self-help book or a fabulous cookbook, the choices are endless.

Visit an art gallery, museum or exhibition

Intimately engaging with other visual art forms can be super inspiring and thought-provoking. Personally, I thoroughly enjoy studying how painters play with light and colour and I take as many mental notes as I can when I look at their work. Exhibitions showing landscape, portrait or wildlife photography are really inspiring too. Strolling through museums can be energetically replenishing and always gets my creative juices flowing. I highly recommend it!

Collaborating with other creatives

Every time I've collaborated with other creative souls, I've walked away from the session feeling like a million dollars: creatively nourished and inspired to the brim. There is something so powerful about coming together and exchanging ideas, sharing experiences and jointly shaping a food scene into something more than you could ever have achieved on your own. Being around other food and photography enthusiasts is like seeing food through their eyes, noticing things you may never have noticed before and finding renewed joy in the simplest parts of the creative process. Because I have witnessed how inspiring collaborations are, I host in-person food photography workshops throughout the year.

NOTE You can find out more about my workshops here: thelittleplantation.co.uk/food-photography-workshops.

Online inspiration: lighter bites only

I love visual platforms, such as Instagram and Pinterest, and wouldn't want to live without them. They've enabled us to build thriving online communities for creative spirits like you and me, and made it easy for us to access and enjoy images whenever we want, wherever we want. But when it comes to using them as a source of inspiration, I'd consume lightly. Don't worry – I'm not banning you from Pinterest picnics, I'm just recommending lighter bites!

Many of the visual social media platforms we love are controlled by algorithms. They tend to continuously feed us images based on what we've viewed before, rather than providing us with new sources of visual inspiration. In addition, they're showing us the same types of imagery as everyone else, leading us to follow trends and create homogeneous-looking food photos instead of finding and fine-tuning our own unique style. There is also the issue of content overload, which can lead to feelings of confusion, overwhelm and comparison, all of which deplete us of creative energy and rob us of inspiration. Furthermore, content overload makes it tricky to know when to stop consuming and start creating content. These platforms offer little space for us to pause and reflect on how we truly feel about the visual information we're presented with. That's why I recommend drawing inspiration from online platforms in tiny doses only – think little nibbles rather than long, drawn-out lunches.

USING INSPIRATION TO HONE YOUR STYLE

So, you've flicked through that awesome cookbook, gone for an invigorating mountain walk and had lunch at the new restaurant everyone is raving about: how is that going to help you find your style and train your photographic eye? Reflect on your experiences and take note of the things that made you smile.

Asking yourself the following questions may also help you along the way:

- What image or moment of your experience was most memorable and inspiring?

- What about it did you find beautiful (or delicious) and is there anything you can take away and apply in your own photography?

- Can you identify which recurring visual themes stood out?

- What failed to inspire you and why?

- What do you notice that changes in your photography following an inspiring experience?

....

....

....

....

....

who are you creating for?

Food photography is a tool that allows you to hold on to a special culinary moment, communicate your food story or share a super-delicious meal with the world. The audience we have in mind for the final image is fundamental to how we take that shot, because not every image we capture will appeal to everyone. Consequently, being clear from the outset whose emotions your image is intended to stir plays a pivotal role in your planning process. Let's look at who your food photography could be aimed at, and how this will affect your creative approach.

Creating for you

When I shoot and style food images with the sole purpose of making my own heart sing, I feel I'm at my most relaxed and adventurous. In those situations, I delve deep into playing with colours, textures, light and angles, even if I'm shooting everyday foods, often unsung culinary heroes that are unlikely to be received by a raving audience online (pots of sauerkraut or a simple veggie broth, anyone?). It's a total luxury to shoot images just for myself and something I'm always keen to make more time and space for. That's because this provides me with the opportunity for study, reflection and exploration without boundaries, time pressures or expectations. Creating with my heart's desires front and centre is so liberating, and one of the many ways I replenish my reserves of creativity and inspiration. Sometimes the end result is an image so personal or unpolished that I would never share it with the wider world. On other occasions, I'm eager to discover whether it will resonate with my audience in the same way it did with me, and consequently put it out there for everyone to see. If, indeed, the image makes my audience happy, I consider it a bonus. However, if the image tanks, I'm usually pretty OK about it. After all, it already fulfilled its primary purpose: it made *me* smile.

Creating for yourself can be a great way to hone your style or find your stride. It's an opportunity to practise your food photography skills and grow in confidence before you share your work with the world.

Creating for your audience

Sharing your food photography with an audience is an act of bravery. You're opening up your creative self to feedback, both good and bad. You run the risk of having the work you poured your heart and soul into be completely ignored. But when your food images connect with an audience and get a heartfelt response, the experience of sharing your photography can be indescribably invigorating and rewarding. Creating food images that captivate the hearts of an audience is, undeniably, an incredible skill, and continuously producing content that resonates is a fine art in and of itself!

If you're creating for an audience, tuning into external feedback is key. Take note of the images you shoot that perform best as well as the ones that fall flat. Doing so will give you endless clues about your audience and allow you to get a better understanding of who you're sharing your images with: what they like, what they dislike and what they want more of. If you are eager to find commercial success, thrive on external affirmation or simply want to make your audience happy, producing more of the type of content you know your audience loves can be the key. Taking a formulaic approach to your food photography while still keeping your imagery exciting, fresh and lush can be a tough balance to strike, but the food photographers who achieve this are the ones who take home the prize.

Creating for a client

Like the process of shooting food images for an audience, creating for clients means you're putting someone else's preferences and expectations first. Instead of doing what makes your heart sing, shooting content for clients is all about bringing their vision to life and making *their* hearts sing. Does this mean you push your sense of style to one side? Absolutely not! Clients come to you because they love the work you've already put out into the world, and they want nothing more than for you to inject some of your creative flair into their images, too!

Creating food photos for clients is as much about honouring their vision as it is about determining how much of your style you sprinkle into the images you shoot for them. It's about listening and gently guiding your clients to identify what they want, while simultaneously adding the final touches to their images in the way that only you can.

Every client project is different, and how far the pendulum swings towards your client's vision versus your own unique style will depend on the client and the project at hand. To ensure you get the balance right, it's crucial you clearly establish what their hopes and visions are for the project by going through a detailed mood board. We'll look at mood board creation in much more detail in much more detail on pages 88–92.

two

PLANNING
A SHOOT

planning a shoot

If you're anything like me, you love browsing through a good cookbook or glossy food magazine. Before I became a full-time food photographer, I'd gaze at those food photos and see effortless deliciousness. Now, having worked behind the scenes of busy cookbook shoots, I know that making food look beautiful and drool-worthy takes a lot of planning, thought and intention. In fact, the more you plan and set your intention for a shoot from the outset, the prettier and more powerful your images will be.

Of course, there are occasions in which a quick iPhone snap will knock it out of the park, but those situations are quite rare, especially if you're at the start of your food photography journey. It's usually the thoughtful, meticulous photographers that reap the rewards and take home a memory card full of the most stunning images ever. In fact, I'd bet my bottom dollar that the photographers whose work you admire most plan their food shoots down to a T!

Planning your shoot means you have a clear roadmap that will help you get to your dream destination, where one shot after another will be exactly the way you envisaged them (or better!). It also means you know exactly what to do when things go pear-shaped. Planning gives you focus, purpose and clarity and frees up vital energy, which you can then pour wholeheartedly into your creative process.

If you walk into a photo shoot, no matter whether you're snapping images for yourself or for a client, with your sights set on a strong, visual end goal, you'll feel more confident, more empowered, more creative. You'll know at what angles to shoot, how to work the light, which props to have at the ready and the order in which you'll take the shots. You'll also have the freedom to be more explorative, because you'll have laid a foundation that is strong enough to cope with a last-minute, bold, adventurous, unique twist. Rather than expending nervous energy trying to figure out what to shoot next or running to the grocery store to pick up that key food item you forgot, you can be present, in the moment, to fine-tune the set-up you've created and make the food on that wonderful ceramic plate really shine!

The more you plan, the more time you will save during the actual shoot. If you've got a lot on your plate (no pun intended) or need to capture that final image before the sun goes down, having the time to spend on the things that take your food photo from 'all right' to breath-taking, is *everything*.

Your ability to plan a shoot with razor-sharp focus and heartfelt intention will make your career as a food photographer more fruitful; it will allow for your photo shoots to run more smoothly, and will put you in the best position to have happy and returning food photography clients. Remember that, in your role as a professional food photographer, you're likely to be part of a team, a group of creatives who will breathe life into food images together. Shooting as a team requires that you guide that collective creative force towards the same drool-worthy vision. That's where planning comes into its own and does the heavy lifting for you.

Planning gives me the time, space and mindset required to be as creative as I can be, and I know it can do the same for you, too! With that in mind, let's look at what to consider.

every image tells a story

'What's the food story you want to tell?'

That's usually the very first question I ask the students who come to study with me. It's a question we discuss in depth, long before we even pick up our cameras or capture a single image. It is the essential first step in the process. It gives our whole process meaning and direction. If you've never thought of your photography in this way before, let's begin with understanding what I mean by a 'food story'.

The way you style, compose and shoot an image of food will always tell a story: it will say something about the dish, and perhaps something about the season or the setting – it will convey a message, always. It might tell the audience that pears dripping with syrup are the only real way to treat yourself on a cold winter's evening, or perhaps that food is best enjoyed in good company. Food photography is ripe for storytelling.

As a plant-based home cook and lover of seasonal deliciousness, a lot of my own photography is focused on the abundance of what Mother Nature gives us; that's the underlying theme of many of my food stories. I want to show seasonal bounty, scrumptious natural ingredients and the generosity that is possible with creating, sharing and eating food. Each individual shot will also have its own narrative: the juiciness of a freshly picked cherry, the joy that comes from the perfect dipping sauce, the happy (and messy!) chaos of baking in a natural, imperfect way. Finding out what food means to you, how you relate to it and the special place it occupies in your heart, will all give shape to your own food stories and enable you to create more authentic, noteworthy images.

When you create, it's important to own that narrative, to ensure that your shot tells the story you want it to, evokes the emotion you desire and, of course, has the impact you are aiming for, particularly if you're shooting commercially.

Why tell a food story?

Sometimes all we want to do is snap a simple, beautiful image of a food or beverage and have that be the end of it. If that's your aim, that's awesome and I say, go for it! But my guess is you picked up this book because you want to photograph food in a way that stands out, evokes an emotion, stirs a food memory and/or seriously causes your audience to drool. Food photography that tells a story has the power to do that. It also provides space for you to inject your style and personality into the image, giving your photography your signature look.

Knowing what you want to communicate with your photography will also help you immensely in planning your shoot and will make it much more likely that the photo you ultimately create has the right impact and achieves its purpose in the world.

'...photograph food in a way that stands out, evokes an *emotion*, stirs a food *memory* and seriously causes your audience to drool.'

TELLING YOUR FOOD STORY: WHERE TO START

Although every shoot is a little different, and it's perfectly fine to give yourself as much flexibility as you need, it's worth asking yourself these questions and using them as your guide *before* you start shooting:

- Who is the audience for this photo? Where will it appear and in what format?

- What does this photograph need to achieve? Is it for pleasure or does it have commercial focus?

- What dish/food/beverage am I photographing today?

- Does the food or beverage have certain qualities that I want to show my audience?

- Do I want to communicate anything about how this dish was made?

- Would I like to transport my viewer to a certain time, season or place?

- Do I wish to share the mood of the moment and if so, what is it?

- What emotion do I want to evoke in my audience?

- Do I solely intend to tell a story about the actual food/dish/beverage, or do I also want to share more about my relationship with the food, how I enjoy it and how I'd recommend my audience enjoys it, too?

- Are there any other details I want my image to highlight?

 NOTE Asking yourself these questions is like giving yourself signposts that will enable your food image to speak more than a thousand words. I've created a downloadable PDF with these questions for you to work through before you embark on your next shoot. If you'd find it helpful, you can get it here: thelittleplantation.co.uk/food-photography-shoot-plan.

SAME FOOD, DIFFERENT STORY

When I baked these vegan banana blondies I wanted to have a play and see if I could capture them in three completely different ways. To do so, I gave one quite an Autumnal feel, I made the other be all about the excitement of grabbing a slice and the final one shot was about putting the blondies front and centre. Which of these images is closest to the story you want to tell? .

GIVE YOURSELF CREATIVE FREEDOM

If, during the shoot, you want to shift gears and tell a different story, that's no problem at all. Creative flexibility is a wonderful thing and allowing yourself to be inspired in the moment can often produce the best kind of imagery. If this happens, revisit the questions above and check that you're doing all you can to tell your new food story in the best way possible.

E. S. TAYLOR & Co.
TATE AGENTS
Tel. 154
3 Hastings Road
Established 1892
DOUGLAS L. SINNATT.

This angle and mood really draw us into the frame.

Here our anticipation builds as we wait for the strawberries to be served with that delicious cake!

STORYTELLING WITH MULTIPLE IMAGES

As we have seen, stand-alone images can speak volumes, but what if you were given the space to tell your food story using multiple images? You may have already taken this opportunity if you've ever shot a recipe from start to finish for your blog, or if you're sharing your work on social media platforms like Instagram. Shooting multiple images is also a scenario you'll encounter if you're asked to share an entire food story in a magazine. It will definitely happen if you shoot a cookbook, where countless images come together to convey the ultimate food story.

I'd love to give you some visual inspiration here that will empower you to tell engaging food stories with multiple images; stories that build tension, maintain intrigue and lead to a delicious resolution.

every food story needs a star

For a food image to really pop and stand out, it needs a focus: a star attraction with whom your audience can fall in love. Just like a brilliant movie needs an engaging plot and an unforgettable main character to bring it to life, your food photo needs those things too. What you're aiming for is for your audience to be drawn into your image, and for their eyes to naturally gravitate towards the star you wish them to see. Having a star attraction will avoid your audience drifting aimlessly through your photo, getting distracted or feeling uncertain what they should look at or rest their eyes on. Therefore, as you plan your shoot, carefully consider what you want to showcase with your food photo, what you want your audience to see and what you want them to wholeheartedly connect to.

Choosing your star attraction

Remember, you are the creative, the director of the show, the storyteller, the one who calls the shots. Therefore, *you* get to decide who your star attraction will be. Most often than not, it's one particular dish, one recipe, one plate of food that you place front and centre because it's so delicious and deserves to play the lead role. So, when in doubt, start there.

There may of course be occasions where your star attraction is an *ingredient* you love, a *colour* you wish to celebrate, or an *action* you want to showcase.

You may even go so far as to make your star attraction a coming together of hungry friends, breath-taking light and shadow play, an intricate composition or a particularly captivating mood.

As long as you remember where to direct your spotlight and ensure your audience can't help but notice your star attraction, you cannot go wrong.

Here, the little blue jug is strategically leading your eye towards my star attraction, that delicious avocado on toast.

Make your star attraction shine

By defining your star attraction from the outset, most of the other decisions you need to make during the planning process, as well as on the shoot itself, will naturally fall into place. For example, if you know that your aim is to mesmerise your audience with the green colour of your soup, you can be considerably more intentional when choosing your overall colour palette and approach the editing process with razor-sharp clarity.

Likewise, if you intend to cast your freshly prepared breakfast as the main star, you can ensure that you pick the right angles, lighting, stage (hello, backdrops) and cast of supporting actors (aka props) who will empower your star to shine brightly. Knowing where you want to guide your audience's eye also means that decisions around composition will come to you more easily; defining your star attraction will remind you not to place anything in the frame that distracts from your star or makes it look anything other than its very best.

Tell your story through your star

Once you've chosen your leading leek or legume, your dazzling Danish or your captivating capsicum, consider how they support and guide the story you are trying to tell. Keeping your star and your food story at the front of your mind will enable you to make decisions about your colour palette, your light and shadow work, your camera angles and camera settings all the more easily. Let's look at those next.

using colour with intention

Do you have a favourite colour? My guess is you probably do. Have you ever stopped to think about *why* you love a certain colour more than others? Or why your favourite colour is likely to be different to mine? Colours are powerful; they connect to something deep within us, often without us even noticing. As creatives, we need to be aware of the colour choices that get us all fired up, as well as the colours that stir something within the hearts of our audience.

Colours tap into our souls, and our response to them is linked to our upbringing, our emotions, our culture and also simple, current trends. In the context of food photography, colours are, of course, also connected to our taste buds! When we see the colour green, we often think of fresh, light, healthy, plant-based flavours. The vibrancy of the colour of a piece of fruit can make us perceive it as sweeter, fresher and more delicious. In fact, the connection between colour and taste is so strong that there are huge, thriving businesses built solely around it: the food colouring industry!

Every colour tells a different story, sets a different scene and evokes a different emotion. Just as you need to be clear from the outset about the story you want to tell, the scene you want to set and the emotion you want to evoke, planning out your colours is crucial to reaching the end result you're after and creating those stand-out images.

So, how do we know which colours to choose? How do we decide which colours go together? How can we ensure that the colours we select in our food photography actually evoke the emotions and tell the story we want them to?

Here's where colour theory and the colour wheel can help us think through and plan which colour(s) we'll use during a shoot, and how to make colour choices that will create the impactful, eye-catching images we're after!

CREATIVITY RULES!

THERE IS NO RIGHT OR WRONG way to combine colours. Everything and anything is possible if it makes your heart sing. Always check in with yourself to see if the colours you're using make you smile or evoke the feeling you want.

BE CLEAR FROM THE OUTSET what you want your image to say. This will help you make better colour-combining decisions. Once you understand the colour wheel, you can plan with even more certainty.

Don't feel the need to limit yourself, particularly if you're just starting out: **THE SKY'S THE LIMIT!**

PLAY AND EXPLORE. Make a note when you're especially happy with the colours you've chosen, so you can learn as you go.

Using the colour wheel to plan your shoot

The colour wheel gorgeously illustrates where colours sit in relation to one another and gives us an easy, visual reference point to draw on when we need to start thinking about colour combining and visual storytelling. It's a great idea to have the colour wheel pinned to the wall and look at it closely before you start your shoot. Then ask yourself the key questions overleaf.

Certain colour choices will naturally and more easily allow you to tell the story you want to tell. Please feel free to use your intuition and let it guide you. Ask yourself if your image should lean towards fresh, vibrant and clean, or perhaps earthy, rustic and muted. Anything is possible.

BEFORE YOU START

MY STARTING POINT?

Perhaps you're about to bake some brownies and know you want to capture the finished product, or perhaps you've grown your very own carrots and want to share your achievement with the world. Maybe you've been asked to shoot an image for a brand and they want you to include their core brand colours. Whatever colour(s) define your star attraction or the brand you intend to capture, make that your starting point!

WHAT'S THE COLOUR TEMPERATURE?

If you draw an imaginary line through the colour wheel, dividing it in half, one side shows all the warm colours and the other side shows the cooler tones. Where does your starting point naturally fall? Does it sit in the warmer spectrum, where colours are vibrant and rich, or does it contain cooler tones, that feel more serene?

These first two questions give you your colour starting point. You can further inform your colour play by reminding yourself of the impact you want to make with your image.

HOW DO I WANT MY IMAGE TO FEEL?

You've already established this in **Every food image tells a story** (page 39), so remind yourself and consider it through the lens of colour. When someone looks at your image, how would you like them to respond? Does that emotion lend itself to a particular colour combination or colour intensity? Trust your instincts here and keep the intended emotion in mind. If your final image evokes that feeling in you, you've nailed it!

Colour combining to create mood

You've got your main colour(s), your starting point, and you know where they sit on the colour wheel. Now the question is, what colour(s) do you add – if any – to create that 'wow' factor, and evoke all the 'feels' in your audience? On the following pages you'll find some suggestions on how to combine colours that will help you shoot stand-out images. However, which of the colour-combining options you'll ultimately choose is completely up to you, because you're the creative and you call the shots. There is no right or wrong way to combine colours: it's all about what makes your heart sing, what defines your style and what you feel is right for your audience.

COMBINING WARM TONES

If your main colour is warm, you can choose to combine it with other warm colours in your backdrops, props or other foods, and in doing so create a scene that feels vibrant or earthy.

Feeling: Warm food images often feel inviting, slightly nostalgic and very grounded.

COMBINING COOLER TONES

If you're working with a cool colour, combining it with other cool colours will create a serene scene that feels calm and fresh.

Feeling: This can be perfect if you want your image to feel crisp, clean and serene.

USING MONOCHROME COLOURS

Keeping your colour palette monochromatic, where you're using just one colour and working with it in a host of different shades and tints, creates a very elegant food photo that puts an undeniable emphasis on that one colour.

Feeling: Monochromatic colour schemes give images a sense of focus and unity, while giving textures and shades in your shot much deeper meaning.

USING ANALOGOUS COLOURS

Using an analogous colour scheme involves using three neighbouring colours, which makes for a well-rounded look that is pleasing to the eye. It's an understated, quietly confident colour palette.

Feeling: This can be perfect if you want your image to feel serene, comfortable and harmonious while injecting a touch of contrast and sense of adventure.

USING COMPLEMENTARY COLOURS

A complementary colour scheme involves using two colours positioned opposite one another on the colour wheel. This makes a more dramatic, bolder statement than using analogue colours. It's a very eye-catching way of using colour because there's so much contrast!

Feeling: This can be perfect if you want to evoke a feeling of excitement and energy.

USING TRIADIC COLOURS

A triadic colour scheme uses three colours that are connected by drawing an equal-sided triangle inside the colour wheel. Not unlike split complementary colours, triadic colour schemes bring harmony *and* contrast to an image. How cool (or warm) is that?

Feeling: The emotional feeling of your colour scheme will be driven by the most dominant colour in your colour palette.

USING SPLIT COMPLEMENTARY COLOURS

This scheme draws on contrast, obtained from using complementary colours, and adding an analogous colour into the mix to increase harmony. This softens the blow of the contrast, creating something impactful yet fluid.

Feeling: This colour scheme is perfect for creatives who love making bold and brave colour choices while creating a beautiful balanced colour palette.

USING THE RAINBOW

Sometimes it's nice to push colour theory aside and just have a wild play, like a toddler discovering finger paint for the first time. Using numerous colours in your image means that it will be hard for one, colour or theme to stand out, but as an overall effect it can still be really powerful. For example, the image below shouts delicious, healthy and vibrant food, giving your audience a sense of abundance.

Feeling: Using an array of colours in your food image is freeing and fun!

BLACK AND WHITE

Black and white aren't colours per se. Instead, black appears when all colours are completely absorbed, which is why it sits on the edge of the colour wheel.

In turn, we perceive something as white when all colour pigments are reflected; therefore, white sits at the centre of the colour wheel. As neither black nor white is tied to one specific colour, we have the freedom to use them in combination with any colour we choose. Their incorporation into a food image will appear seamless. That's why I look at black and white as neutrals that go with pretty much everything!

White is wonderful as a base on which to place colourful food (think yogurt, white rice, white plates and white backdrops, etc.), allowing it to pop and seriously stand out. Using white can create a very uplifting, light and cheerful mood in your food photography. In contrast, black is great as a base or backdrop when you want to create darker images with a moody, mysterious or cosy feel.

NOTE Editing colours: Sometimes the way you edit an image can really allow your colours to shine. Perhaps you're using warm colours because that's what's available, but you actually want to give everything a cooler tone? You can still achieve that by playing with your white balance and tone curves in editing. We'll talk about editing on pages 185–195.

Play with your palette

As I've said before, there is no single correct way to use colours, and there's no single colour or particular colour palette that can work for every possible food scene you'll ever want to create. Instead it's about being mindful of which colour(s) make up your starting point, how these colours will react to the light you have available (more on that in the next section), which colour combinations make your heart sing, the story that you want to tell and who you're telling it to. Within that, as always, there's ample room to explore and play. So, embrace those colours, allow your personal style and preferences to reveal themselves as you play, and enjoy the technicolour ride!

finding your light

I want you to look at light as a living thing because, well, it behaves like one. It has the power to transform, to bring life, and to literally brighten up any day. When it comes to food photography, light is the secret sauce. You want to be able to capture that light in all its glory and make it work to your benefit. Moreover, you want to make the most of the interplay between light, shadow and the food you wish to capture, because that's where the magic happens!

To be intentional about telling your story and creating the image you want, you need to become a master of light and carefully use it to convey just the right message. That takes a little planning – and a lot of play. Discovering when and where to shoot to consistently get the best results will save you so much time, not only in the setting up of each shot, but also after you've captured the image. To the surprise of many of my students, I do relatively little post-editing on my images. That's because I truly believe the magic lies in dancing with the light from the outset and capturing it with your camera; it will not only save you time on editing, it will also infuse your work with a noticeable quality and glow.

Sunlight is constantly changing, so how on earth do you find 'your' light, the one that's right for your unique style of food photography? Let's look at what affects light and how, through a little experimentation, you can get a feel for your perfect light.

'...the magic lies in *dancing with the light* from the outset and capturing it with your camera.'

Time of day

Light changes depending on the time of the day. An extreme example is to think of the lack of light at midnight and the presence of daylight at noon. But between these two extremes, as the light transitions from night to day and back, there are many different variations.

So, how do you know when is the best time of the day for you to photograph your food and, moreover, does timing really matter?

I like capturing the crisp morning light but in order to know when the light is best for you, try and shoot your food at different times throughout the day. Make a note of when you took each shot, then compare your images and see which ones make your food look lush, delicious and noteworthy! You'll soon realise that the time of day at which you shoot your food matters a lot, and you'll begin to get a sense of what time is the right time for you.

SPRING/SUMMER

AUTUMN/WINTER

Time of year

As the seasons change, the relationship between the Earth and the sun changes, too. In the winter, when the hemisphere we are in is tilted away from the sun, we have shorter, darker days. During the summer, when the hemisphere we are in is tilted towards the sun, we have longer, brighter days. In summer in the UK, I can shoot using natural daylight until 8 p.m. without any problems.

The colour and temperature of light also varies depending on the season. In the summer, the light is quite warm, veering towards yellow. In the winter, it is cooler and bluer. All of these small differences can have a massive impact on the feeling and quality of your food photos.

So, it's worth discovering in which season you prefer to shoot your food, and at what time of day your preferred season's light is at its best. If there is a season that's really tricky to shoot in, note down the times of day at which you *can* make the season's light work for you and harness those shooting opportunities!

NOTE I have a super-helpful template you can download from my blog that will allow you to make notes on your light throughout the day and during different seasons. You can find it here: thelittleplantation.co.uk/best-food-photography-lighting.

Your location

I once worked remotely with a student in the Middle East. She noted that she'd love to create the cool, moody food images she saw photographers in Scandinavia produce. Although there are lots of things she could do to produce that same look and feel, the reality is that for most of the day, the light available to her would result in very different images to those she sees taken by a food bloggers in, say, Finland. That's because the Middle East is closer to the equator, where sun's rays are warmer and more abundant.

In short, your location will have a big impact on your food photos. I recommend you play to the beauty of the light you're surrounded by.

Living and working in London means that my home studio is usually filled with soft, diffused light.

The direction your window faces

In what direction does the window in your chosen shooting space face? North, south, east, west or somewhere in between? Knowing the exact answer will enable you to unlock and enhance the full potential of the light and shadow play available to you. It will also give you a better understanding of how light travels into your studio space and help you predict optimal shooting times.

For example, if you live in the northern hemisphere, a north-facing window means there is never any direct sunlight, so your food will be bathed in indirect light. A south-facing window can be fabulous for shooting food early in the morning and also later in the afternoon if you're eager to avoid harsh sunlight, but you might struggle in the middle of the day.

Free floating light

I always like to imagine light as little, free-floating particles, that are eager to caress your food and make it shine. If their pathway is obstructed by a tall fence, a big tree or anything else that blocks the window into your studio space, this will greatly affect the quality of your photo. So, choose a shooting area where those light particles can float freely through the window unhindered; it will make all the difference.

Distance to light source

Let's stay with this image of free-floating light particles, shall we? Imagine that you have set up your shooting area and the light particles are full of life, ready to illuminate your food. But if the food you are photographing is too far away from your light source, those very particles will need to travel quite some distance, losing their power, energy and impact, in turn leaving your food looking lacklustre. So, for the best results, ensure your shooting surface is really close to, and on the same level as, the window or door you're using as your light source!

Size matters!

Well, it does in food photography. If your window is big and allows lots of light into your studio space, this will create rather different images than if you have a tiny window that restricts light flow. Both can work beautifully, but the bigger the window, the more flexibility you've got. My window is rather large, flooding my studio with natural light. This means that, even in low light conditions, I usually have quite a bit of light available to make a shot work. In turn, if I want to create a really dramatic, dark and moody look, I can cover parts of my window and allow less light into the studio, which makes for gorgeous images. So, if at all possible, choose a shooting space with a larger window, so you have more freedom to play with light.

Your space

The colour and height of the ceiling, and the texture and colour of the floor and walls of the space where you take your pictures will have a significant impact on the look and feel of your photos. Is your shooting space light and bright or dark and cosy? All these seemingly tiny details matter so much because the ceilings, walls and floors – essentially the room as a whole – all act as reflectors or absorbers of light!

My studio space (and most food photography studios I know) has white walls, allowing the light particles to float and bounce around, and moveable polystyrene foam walls that are white on one side and black on the other (for moodier shots).

Please be careful if shooting in a space with walls that are yellow, pink, orange or red: colourful walls may 'throw off' the real colours of the food you are shooting. This is almost impossible to fix, even in post-processing.

NOTE You and your body, as well as the backdrop you shoot on, will act as reflectors and absorbers of light, too, especially if you shoot hand-held. Consequently, think carefully about the colours of the clothes you wear during a shoot, as it will have a big impact on the end result.

WHEN THE LIGHT JUST ISN'T THERE: A NOTE ON ARTIFICIAL LIGHT PHOTOGRAPHY

In case it's not blatantly obvious, I love the challenge of finding, dancing and playing with ever-changing, beautiful natural light. I'm also blessed with a home studio that is flooded with gorgeous natural light and hence I've not felt the urge to use artificial light for my own food photography.

However, I know that some of you won't be able to photograph your food during daylight hours, and/or don't have a shooting space with adequate natural light available to you. If that's you, using artificial lights, designed for (food) photography, may be the way to go.

Although I won't be exploring your artificial light options here, what I can advise is the following:

DO YOUR RESEARCH. Not all artificial photography lights are created equal. The light source you choose (continuous lighting, flash or both) and the brand you opt for will greatly impact the look and feel of your photos.

SEE WHAT YOU LIKE. Follow the work of artificial light food photographers. Find out about their lighting set-up and take it from there.

BUDGET FOR EXTRAS. You may need to purchase a few extras, like scrims and umbrellas. Budget for them accordingly.

THE ADVICE ON LIGHT IN THIS BOOK IS STILL HELPFUL! The areas we are going to cover later, such as looking for your light and shadow points and thinking of your light's direction, are as relevant when working with artificial light as they are with natural light.

WORK WITH WHAT YOU'VE GOT. Images taken with artificial light have a different look and feel to those shot with natural light. Flash food photography in particular can look really dramatic (and – I think – cool). Rather than trying to make your artificial light shots look like they were taken using natural light, roll with it and milk it for what it's worth.

Finding your light is worth the effort

It might take you a little bit of time to find just the right spot that gives you the perfect light, but it's worth taking that time to find it in advance. Make this part of your pre-planning process to save you time and energy on shoot day.

Your perfect set-up might even entail changing things around as the sun moves, the seasons change or the story you want to tell (or how you want to tell it) evolves. Remember to reassess and double check your lighting throughout the shoot to ensure it's still allowing you to capture your food in the best way possible. I know this sounds like a lot of work but I promise you:

All the *time* and *effort* you put into finding your light will be totally worth it!

camera angles

If you've ever taken a selfie or had your portrait shot, you'll know that getting the angle right matters. It's no different when we think about showcasing your star attraction: there will be some angles that are super flattering and work really well and some, not so much. It's your role as a food photographer to pick the right one and make your star attraction look a million dollars.

Mastering camera angles has been key in moving my career from shooting solely for social media platforms, to working full-time as a food photographer. Getting to grips with angles showcases your skill, your creativity and your ability to uniquely approach each and every star attraction in just the right way.

Now, I wish I could tell you that I decide on camera angles in the spur of the moment, making it up as I go along. But the truth is, as with everything else, I enter my shoot with a clear idea in mind. That includes thoroughly thinking through which camera angles will showcase my star beautifully and make it look utterly drool-worthy. Sure, there's *always* space for spontaneity – but paradoxically, planning out my shooting angles allows more creative play to occur because I've taken the burden of making big decisions off my shoulders and can focus on the finer, fun details during the shoot instead.

Like everything else you read in this book, please know there is no one correct angle in food photography. It would be dull if there were! However, there are most certainly ways to optimise your food photos by choosing the most advantageous angles for your particular star attraction. Here are the fundamentals you need to bear in mind in order to tell your story in the most beautiful way possible...

Shooting from above with a wide-angle lens, can give your audience a deeper understanding of your image's story and context.

Choosing the angle

Before I even pick up my camera, I study the dish I have created closely to establish what angle will showcase its deliciousness to the max and allow me to share the food story I want with the world.

I think carefully about:

- the type of food or scene I am photographing.
- which key feature(s) I wish to highlight and draw awareness to.

Then I am able to explore which angles will work best in showcasing my star and telling my food story.

SHOOTING FROM ABOVE

Most star attractions look *fabulous* when shot from a bird's-eye perspective, making it a very popular shooting angle in food photography. Shooting your food from above enables you to show off the entire dish, as well as introduce key story telling elements and – if you're so inclined – a killer composition!

Foods that look the bomb when shot from above include salads, bowl food, platters, pizzas, pies, pasta and noodle dishes and open-faced sandwiches. Really, any food whose most interesting features – be they colours, textures, garnishes, etc. – can be best appreciated from a bird's-eye perspective should be shot at this angle. There are *very* few foods that don't work when shot from above so, if in doubt, start here.

SHOOTING AT AN ANGLE

I would call anything between 90 and 0 degrees an angle. It's a *huge* range, giving you so many different options to tell your food story. How high or low you take that shot is up to you! You're the artist and you get to decide.

SHOOTING HIGHS AND LOWS

Drinks and foods that offer a little height and have beautiful and delicious details can look ace at a 45-degree angle or lower.

Star attractions that lack height love it when the camera is held a little higher, above 45 degrees. But please remember, there are no set rules: so experiment, play and see what you like best.

KEEP IT INTERESTING

When shooting at an angle, why not think outside the box? In the first image here, I took the shot at an angle of around 45 degrees, but included the model's arm and shoulder to add interest and a hint of storytelling. This put my star attraction – that delicious chocolate sauce – in the context of how (and by whom) it was being prepared.

In the second shot, I held the camera really high (by standing on a stool), ignoring all straight lines to shoot at a 75-degree angle for added detail and context.

SHOOTING STRAIGHT/SIDE-ON

Last but not least, you've got the option of shooting your food scene with your camera held dead straight, capturing your star attraction from the side! This angle works wonders when you're shooting drinks, layer cakes, stacked food (like piles of pancakes, or heaps of brownies), or anything else with height. It's so lovely shooting at this angle if your star attraction has interesting details that can only be seen from this perspective, be it a colourful stripy straw in a drink or beautiful, silky layers in a breakfast parfait. Shooting from this angle can also work well if you're trying to capture motion.

CLOSE-UP: YOUR STAR ATTRACTION IN FOCUS

When I teach my food photography workshops and online courses, I always ask my students to take at least one close-up shot. That's because, in the heat of the moment, taken up with food styling and composition, we sometimes forget to focus on the little details. And it is precisely these little details that close-up shots capture so beautifully.

To make your star attraction shine in a close-up shot:

- Choose a food that is naturally beautiful, with interesting textures and colour.

- Keep your shot *super* minimal, without props and added extras.

- Shoot one ingredient rather than a complete, final dish.

- Consider shooting your chosen ingredient in abundance.

- Use your macro lens for the best possible results.

- Avoid holding your camera too close to your subject. Give your star breathing space and your camera an opportunity to focus correctly.

When planning, decide in advance which angles you'd like to feature in your food story. Of course, you will always have the freedom to add in more angles, or fewer, but having a place to start saves time and enables you to jump into your shoot with clarity and purpose.

NOTE On my website I have pulled together the considerations outlined here and created a worksheet for you to download and take to a shoot. You can download one here: thelittleplantation.co.uk/best-food-photography-camera-angles.

creating a mood board

Your mood board is a gorgeous arrangement of ideas. It will contain photographs of all the creative elements and considerations you have thought about up until now. Your mood board will allow you to plan and execute your shoot with purpose. It will help you to identify (and offer you a reminder of) the mood you wish to convey, the story you hope to tell, the colours you want to include, the angles you intend to shoot at and the frames you aim to capture. In short, your mood board will help you streamline your planning process and guide your shoot seamlessly towards your end goal.

Mood boards are so helpful that I'd argue you should *always* use them, even if you're working on a small (un)paid solo project, or when you are 'just' shooting something for yourself (or, who are we kidding here, for Instagram). A mood board is particularly valuable if you're collaborating with a team or completing work for a paying client. It can also be a lifesaver if you're on a super-tight schedule. In these scenarios, a mood board can minimise the chances of creative disagreements and disappointments, instead guiding everyone in the same direction, providing structure as well as a clear, joint visual focus.

Mood board creation takes practice and skill but, once mastered, it can make the shooting process considerably easier and faster, more efficient and more fun. Plus, with the mood board there to provide solid scaffolding, you can let your creativity run free and your own unique style shine through. So, let's get to the mood boarding process.

WHAT TO INCLUDE IN A MOOD BOARD

COLOURS

Your colour palette is a key part of your mood board. Once it is at the ready, it's there for you to refer back to as you shop for food ingredients, choose your props, etc.

MOOD

The mood board should clearly show the mood and feeling you aim to capture.

ANGLES AND FRAMES

To avoid taking a hundred shots that look exactly the same, carefully consider from which angles you wish to shoot and how you want to frame your food. Include images that encapsulate your vision.

BACKDROPS

Your mood board should, ideally, contain a shot that shows your chosen backdrop(s), or ones that are similar. We will explore this in **Backdrop selection** on page 123.

PROPS

Include a few images that have props similar in style to the ones you intend to use. You'll find more detail on props on pages 165–177.

FOOD, STYLING AND COMPOSITION

Your mood board should also feature the dish(es) you wish to capture and the styling and composition of what you're roughly going for.

Sending a client a well-thought-out moodboard makes for a great first impression.

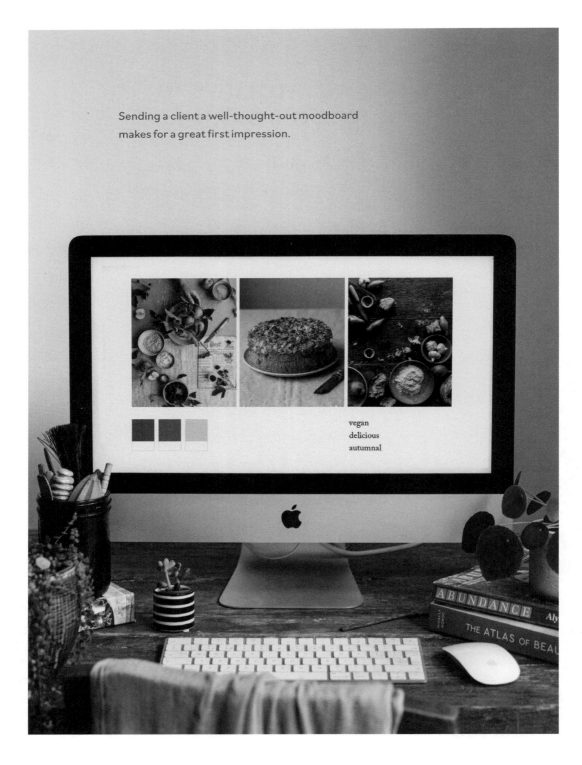

A guiding focus

Your mood board will already be serving you well during your planning stage, but it will really come into its own during the actual photo shoot, when you can refer back to it and ensure you captured all the frames you set out to. During the shoot, your mood board will also provide styling and composition inspiration, which comes in particularly handy if you're feeling creatively stuck. You may not be in a position to plan your first mood board just yet, as you may still need to get to grips with backdrops, props, camera angles and all things styling, so come back to this once you've got to the end of the Styling chapter and you'll be ready to mood board away. I wanted to cover it here, though, because the mood board is such an integral part of the process that you should be considering it the whole time.

I'm so excited for you to see how mood boards will *boost* your food photography flow.

MOOD BOARDS FAQ

HOW MANY IMAGES SHOULD I INCLUDE?

I try to have one or two examples for each shot I intend to capture; this way I have options, without overwhelm.

WHERE DO I SOURCE THE IMAGES FOR MY MOOD BOARD?

I love using Pinterest or Instagram, as they're not only where I can find images, but also where I can create the actual mood board and share it with a client or a team if required. To share the mood board (if Instagram or Pinterest aren't an option), I save images on a PDF and email it over to anyone who needs to see it. If the mood board includes images that aren't mine, I make that abundantly clear and credit the actual photographers whose work I've used as inspiration.

ONCE CREATED, CAN A MOOD BOARD BE ALTERED?

Yes absolutely! It's like a living, breathing thing. If there are images there that don't serve you, remove them to make way for others that do.

Having spent all this time planning and preparing, it's time to pick up our cameras. Are you ready?

your camera, your way

A food photographer with a camera is like a painter with a paintbrush. Your camera is the tool that makes *everything* possible. You can approach it with fear or with curiosity. You can view it as a complicated gadget or recognise it for the wonderful device it is, one which permits you to express your creativity and share it with the world.

Rather than look at your camera through a technical lens, I really want us to focus in on the two incredible superpowers your camera grants you: first, the ability to play with light; and secondly, the opportunity to bring your visual story to life. Keeping these two points at the forefront of your mind as you pick up your camera is what will allow you to move beyond stifling technicalities and towards creative freedom.

NOTE As you're not a complete beginner and this book focuses on creativity rather than camera basics, I did not include an in-depth breakdown of your camera settings, how to move beyond automatic mode or how to get to grips with shutter speed, ISO and aperture (F-stop). However, if you are looking for that, I've got you covered! I have a detailed PDF waiting for you to download here: thelittleplantation.co.uk/how-to-shoot-in-manual-mode. This includes the three key camera functions and how to master them.

Light chaser

Your camera has three main settings: shutter speed, aperture (also referred to as F-stop) and ISO. All three enable you to pull more light into the camera if you wish, flooding the camera's sensor with light, or to push light away, giving your images a completely different feel. You get to decide how much light is too much, or when more is required, depending on the story you want to tell and the mood you want to create. You're the painter, remember: the creative who gets to call the shots. Getting your food photos to look just the way you want is all about how you choreograph these three settings to enable them to dance with one another. In other words, your three camera settings allow you to mould, shape and manipulate the light you are playing with and, as we've already explored in **Finding your Light** (pages 69–79), it's *everything*!

To get the most out of the camera, avoid working on autopilot and always choosing the same old settings. Instead, consider exposing your image perfectly by using the three available settings in the most optimal way. You can achieve this by continuously readjusting and evaluating your light source and your camera settings, and carefully checking the images you're creating.

Is the lighting in the shot just right? Awesome! Is it not quite hitting the mark? Readjust your settings and try again. Working like this means truly immersing yourself in the process, taking full creative control and being intentional about your light and shadow play. It's also a lot of fun!

50MM PRIME LENS
1/125 – F5.6 – ISO320

100MM MACRO LENS
1/100 – F7.1 – ISO400

Creating a mood

I love that two food photographers can shoot exactly the same food scene, but simply by choosing different camera settings and ways of framing their shot, they will produce two totally different images. The most fascinating thing about this is that both images can be perfectly exposed and utterly beautiful, yet still unique. Isn't that fascinating? This happens because two of the settings – shutter speed and aperture – not only allow you to control light and shadow, but also have powerful storytelling properties. The way you frame your shot then completes your signature look.

1/320 - F4.5 - ISO400

This image was shot using double exposure.

Adding movement or that dreamy bokeh

Shutter speed enables you to bring movement into your image, be it blurred or frozen, making your shot come alive and giving your viewer a sense that they are part of the scene, witnessing a precious moment (see pages 96–97).

Your aperture, on the other hand, can produce that dreamy look also referred to as bokeh. Playing with a large aperture will create a beautiful bokeh and allow you to draw the viewer's eye to a particular point in your frame (perhaps your star attraction); a small aperture, by contrast, will make everything razor-sharp and consequently ensure you guide your audience through the entire food scene, inviting them to savour every aspect of it.

As with everything in food photography, what you decide to do with your shutter speed and aperture lies completely in your hands. This means you've got lots of wiggle room for creative expression and telling the story you want to in your own unique signature style.

BOKEH AND MOVEMENT!

Why choose one if you can
have both?

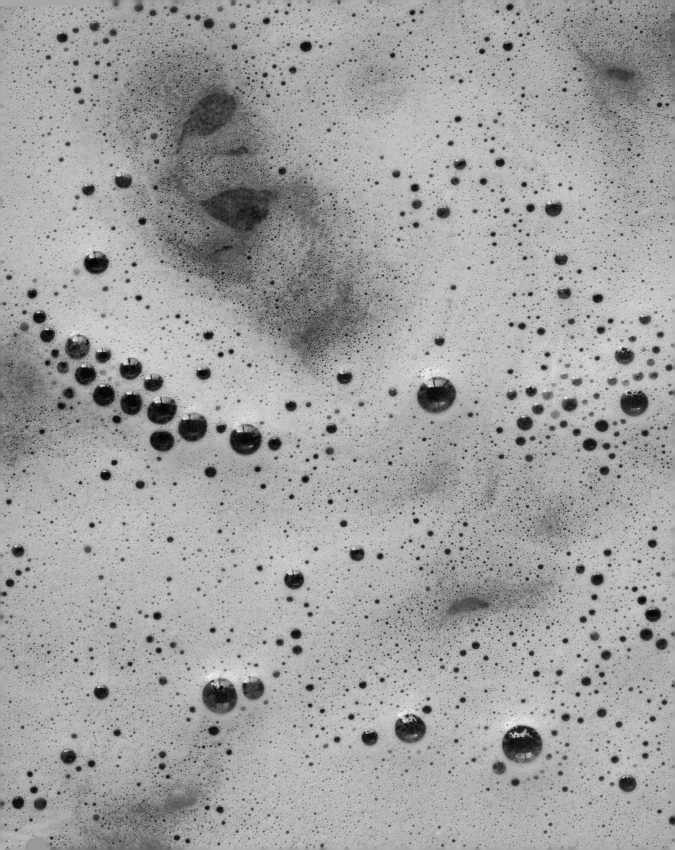

three

SHOOTING YOUR STAR

shooting your star

You've found your light, established your colour palette, planned your shoot, got to grips with the camera settings and angles that create your signature style and have your mood board to hand. With your dish prepared, it's time to let loose your creativity once more and capture that drool-worthy, stand-out image (or three).

It's nearly time to shoot, but first let's *set the stage*.

We need the supporting actors that will really help you showcase your star in style: lighting, props, backdrops, composition and, of course, that all-important styling. These elements add the final touches to your image and are worth looking at more closely, so let's do it!

lighting your star

Remember in **Finding your light** (pages 69–79) I mentioned that working with gorgeous light is fundamental to making your food images look incredible? Light is the key to unlocking the story you want to tell and the feeling you wish to evoke. By now you've explored and tried different shooting spots and found the best one for you. Now you need to ask yourself what light direction you want to work with in order to showcase your star in the best way possible.

Light direction

Let's imagine it's 12 noon on a clear spring day, that you want to work with lots of indirect light, that you have a large north-facing window and live in the northern hemisphere. Bingo! You should be set and ready to take the food images you want, right? Totally – but there is another important element to consider that will really help you get the shot you want, and that's light direction. Where the light source is in relation to your star attraction, or your entire food scene, is super important, but like all things food photography, there isn't just one way to make it work. Let's take a look at all the options available, shall we?

SIDE LIGHT

A great option is side light, where the light hits one side of the subject. I love using side light, especially when I want to capture a big scene. The shot often seems to have a more balanced look, and you get gorgeous shadows towards the side of the food. Side light works for almost any food scene at any angle and creates a rather understated look. Dreamy!

Shadow

Light

Light

Shadow

BACK LIGHT

Is it just me or is back light – where the light hits the back of the food and the food stands between you and the light source – super sexy?! I love using back light to give my shots a more dramatic, edgy look. It works really well with beverages in glasses or clear bottles. I also enjoy using back light if I'm shooting a shallow bowl or a single plate; ideally the food should be of quite a low height, like a pie or an open crepe, so the light particles have more of a chance to work their magic over the entire surface of the food.

I tend to avoid using back light if I'm shooting something with a lot of height, say a layer cake, straight-on. This is because the camera will be focusing in on the shadowy area of the food. It's like giving your star attraction centre stage, then not shining the spotlight on its best side; to my eye it's not very appealing. But as always, explore and see what works for you.

That 90-degree bracket between back light and side light works wonderfully too! It's so fun to have this range to experiment and play with, causing shadows to fall at a really gorgeous diagonal angle.

It's worth exploring this option if neither using strictly side light nor using solely back light is allowing you to showcase your star in the way that makes your heart sing.

Light

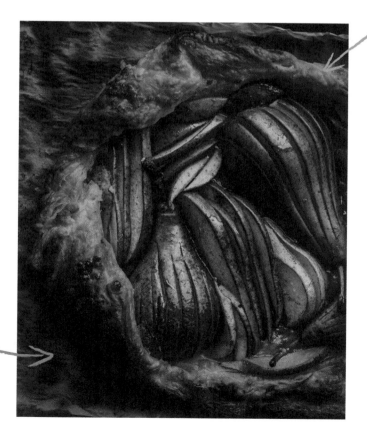

Shadow

BACK LIGHT *AND* SIDE LIGHT

Want to take it a step further? Don't want to choose one, but instead want both? If so, another great option is to have side *and* back light. This set-up occurs naturally if you shoot near bay windows or in corners where there are windows on two sides. Although having two light sources can be fantastic, be mindful that your shadows will be much softer and smaller than if you were shooting with one light source only. This means you need to make sure that your star attraction doesn't look flat. If it does, explore blocking off one of the windows or using a black reflector to balance out your added light flow.

Which light direction should I choose?

So many choices, so little time! Please remember: you're the creative, you get to choose the story you want to tell, and you get to decide what light direction tells that story best. Therefore, which of the four options you go for is totally up to you.

My advice would be:

- Take some test shots using first back and then side light to see which works best.

- Think about where you'd like the light and shadow to fall. Are there any aspects of the food you wish to accentuate?

- If you're shooting drinks, play with back light first.

- If you're shooting anything with lots of height, working with side light is likely to be a better starting point.

- Take the time to play, experiment and explore. See what allows your star attraction to look the most delicious, then go with that.

FOOD LIGHTING NO-NOS

Avoid sky lights, restaurant or kitchen ceiling lights, flashlights on your camera, or any other **LIGHTING THAT HITS THE FOOD FROM ABOVE**. Top light will make your food look very flat and boring as it kills your shadows.

Avoid a situation where light comes from **VARIOUS DIRECTIONS**: think conservatories or certain outdoor picnic shots, where you have light everywhere (see notes on outdoor food photography on page 120). Your light and shadow play will be hard to control, and you run the risk of creating flat images.

Avoid **FRONT LIGHT**, as this will cause your body to create a shadow on the food and stop those all-important light particles from reaching your star attraction.

Avoid **MIXING ARTIFICIAL LIGHT AND NATURAL LIGHT**. It's not impossible to get it right, but it's not recommended. Mixing natural light and artificial light can make it hard to correct and manage your white balance, even in post-processing.

the interplay between light...

Many of the creatives I have taught love the idea of playing with light. In fact, given half a chance, it's not uncommon for them to engulf their food with light, sometimes even over-exposing their image. When I ask them why they are creating such bright shots, they often say that they're worried about having shadows in their food photographs.

Ironically, within the context of food photography, light can only work its magic if it's balanced out by beautiful shadows. In fact, it's actually the interplay between light and shadows that allows your food to look lush, delicious and three dimensional, as opposed to flat. I believe that harnessing the connection between light and shadow is what will take your photos from good to spectacular.

What about the dark side?

Now, you may ask yourself how deep, prominent or long your shadows 'should' be. The tricky thing is that there's no right or wrong answer here: it's really a matter of personal taste. Food photography is art, remember? It's about the story you want to tell, and you get to decide how you tell it.

Personally, I adore playing with deeper shadows, even when I am taking a light and bright photo. I feel it makes food look more alive and real. It's why I often go a step further and accentuate my shadows in post-processing, and it's part of my own signature style. I urge you to boldly explore and experiment with all the light possibilities and to embark on a journey of self-reflection, noting down how darker, more pronounced shadows make you feel. Whatever light and shadow set-up makes your heart sing the loudest, I say, go with that.

...and shadow

What kind of light?

DIFFUSED LIGHT

Most of my food photography images use diffused light, which is when the light particles have been softened, either by clouds (which is true in my case, as I live in rainy London) or any other kind of diffuser. Using diffused light creates a dreamy, airy look, with clearly defined yet soft shadows. I absolutely adore diffused light and it's a look you're probably very familiar with because most food photographers use it as their preferred option. It's a very commercial, timeless look that allows the food to take centre stage.

HARSH LIGHT

Harsh light happens when the sun's rays are strong and powerful, hitting your food directly, without being softened through diffusion. Does this mean you should stay clear of harsh light? Absolutely not! Harsh light can look super intense, utterly stunning and incredibly dramatic: it can really make your image pop. It creates a lot of contrast between light and shadow points in your image and intensifies your food's colours, making a bold and beautiful statement in the process. This kind of light can sometimes dominate an image, though. It's also a little bit like Marmite: some people love it and others can't stand it! .

See overleaf for examples of the same subject shot in both diffused light and harsh light

DIFFUSED LIGHT

HARSH LIGHT

Clients generally prefer images shot using diffused light, but it's worth clarifying this point before embarking on your shoot.

EXPERIMENT TO FIND YOUR WAY

My suggestion is to start exploring the power of light by working with diffused light first. It will give you a really good foundation and understanding of the interplay between light and shadow, and how you can make it work in a way that best conveys your message. It will also enable you to create images that will resonate with a wider audience as well as commercial clients. After you've gained confidence in balancing light and shadow within the context of diffused light, explore working with harsh light, harnessing the lessons you've learned from working with diffused light first.

Do you have harsh lighting conditions in the space you shoot in, but want that dreamy, diffused look? Grab a diffuser and create the soft light you're after, growing in your understanding of the interplay between light and shadow!

TELLING IT AS IT IS

I am always fascinated to see other people's food photography set-ups on social media. Many of them have foam boards, cardboard and reflectors everywhere! I think many of my students must see these rather complicated looking arrangements on social media, too, as their sense of relief is palpable when I show them how I shoot. The vast majority of the time, I don't use reflectors, diffusers, cardboard boxes or *anything* other than natural light and shadows, because I love it when nature does its 'thang'. In all honesty, there's nothing more satisfying to me than when light clings to the food as it wants to and shadows simply appear where they need to. To my eye, it creates a very organic scene that embraces and makes the most of what really *is*. That's the story *I* want to tell, the one that makes *my* heart sing. So, if you're just starting out and unsure of how to bounce light around, I recommend you start with a very simple set-up and see what happens!

USING A REFLECTOR

So, am I dissing reflectors? Absolutely not! They, and the other tools I have mentioned, exist for good reason and may just be the item you need to take your photos to the next level. So, let's think about what a reflector does and how you could use it to enhance your creative work.

A reflector bounces the light in your studio space back on to your star. If you use the white, silver or golden side of your reflector, you're increasing the amount of light flooding your image. This can be great if you're looking to create a bright shot, if you're dealing with very low light conditions and need a little boost of light, or if you wish to lighten a particular, dark, part of your frame.

It can also work well when you're shooting something with height, for example a bundt cake, and wish to illuminate the side that's a tiny bit darker and further away from your light source.

Finally, if you're facing a situation where you have to shoot in lighting conditions that make your food look flat, reflectors can help lift and define your dish a tiny bit more.

The silver and golden-coloured reflectors are more powerful than the solid white ones, and golden reflectors also create a warmer feel. Depending on where, at what angle and how close you place your reflector(s), you will probably also soften the natural shadows in your photo. So, if you're not a fan of deep shadows, working with a white, silver or golden reflector might be just the way to go.

NO REFLECTOR

SILVER REFLECTOR

GOLD REFLECTOR

BLACK REFLECTOR

Creating dark & moody images

Often people have the idea that, in order to create dark images, you need to have little or no natural light; consequently, they under-expose their images. The truth is that the very same principles that we have already discussed about finding and harnessing your light also apply to dark food photography. Just as you do with lighter images, you need a good, natural light source to ensure your food is properly and beautifully lit. What makes an image moodier is not the lack of light, but the supporting actors; your backdrop, colour scheme and prop choice, as well as your camera settings and editing choices, of course.

Now, if you're a bit of a drama queen/king, go ahead and use a black reflector. Depending on where, at what angle and how close you place this to your food, you will deepen the shadows and make your shot moody and mysterious. This is because the black reflector won't actually reflect, but instead absorb light, which is great if you want to tone the light down a bit.

Here's another thing to consider: the smaller the window through which your light comes, the more dramatic your image will get. If, like me, you have quite a large window, consider blocking parts of the window off with cardboard! If nothing else, it is worth experimenting with this; be inquisitive, have fun and see what happens.

The following techniques will also help create moodier shots:

- Use a dark background so that much of the light can be absorbed.
- Use dark props to tell your moody story.
- Don't over or under-expose your image.
- Use a black reflector to create dark shadows.
- Deepen the blacks and shadows when you edit afterwards.

These two images were shot in the exact same location, at the exact same time of the day! The only differences are the model's clothes and the colour of the backdrop.

Outdoor food photography

Compared to shooting in your chosen studio space, it's much harder to control and manipulate the light when photographing food outdoors. This is because you don't have just one or two light sources or windows to contend with: instead, you've got floating light particles everywhere! This means that you need to pay extra attention to the time of day at which you're shooting, as well as your light and shadows, and the movement of the sun!

THE GOLDEN HOUR

A great starting point for your outdoor food photography shots, is to take your pictures during the 'golden hour'. This is the poetic term used to describe the brief time periods shortly after sunrise and shortly before sunset, when the sun's rays are glowing, warm and magical, and the shadows are soft, dreamy and oh-so pretty. This magical effect happens because the sun is low on the horizon and isn't as potent and forceful as it is at other times of day.

As with all food photography set-ups, please make sure that your food is placed so that the sun is behind it (back-lit), beside it (side-lit) or somewhere in between those two points, as outlined earlier in this chapter. Then watch those sun rays shimmer and sparkle over your food.

NOTE The light will forever move and change during the golden hour, so be alert and ready to press the trigger when those light particles are just right!

If you want to photograph food during the golden hour,
factor in the time it will take you to set up your scene.

DURING THE DAY

Let's be honest, photographing your food outdoors during the golden hour isn't always possible. So how do you work with outdoor light the rest of the day? First, stay away from situations where the light is directly above the food (generally, this is just before, during and just after midday) as this will create shadow-less, flat-looking images.

Secondly, watch your shadows: are they falling behind your food, beside it, or somewhere in between? If so, you're all good. Anything else, and it's worth pausing and taking stock.

Thirdly, work that harsh light! If you're shooting outdoors during the height of summer, take advantage of the dramatic harsh light and shadow points! If you *really* don't like that look, bring a diffuser along to your shoot, or choose a different time of day to photograph your food.

Fourthly, if you have to shoot in shadowy corners, pay even closer attention to your food's shadows! Are they present and pretty, or completely MIA? Often, shooting in shadowy areas (next to tall trees or a garden shed, for example) can create very flat-looking images. So, be cautious!

Now that you know how to light your food to perfection in any situation, shall we take a closer look at other key steps you can take to further impact light and shadow, complete your food story and make your star attraction look incredible?

HARSH LIGHT

SHADOWS

When shooting in dark, shadow filled areas, either bring a reflector along to introduce highlights into your image, or try and find spots where light can find its way through, like I did in this shot.

backdrop selection: setting the foundation for your scene

Backdrops – the surfaces you use in your food photos – set the tone of your image and form the foundation on which you build your food scene. They contribute to creating the mood and telling your food story. They also play a huge role in what happens with your light and how all the colours in your image come together. It's for this reason that I turn my attention to choosing my backdrop so early on in the process, essentially right after deciding what my star attraction will be. In this chapter, we'll take a closer look at backdrop selection and its effect on light and shadow play. We'll also explore how to pick the right one for the story you seek to tell. Are you ready?

The choices are endless

There are so many different food photography backdrops for you to choose from, including fabrics, wood, stone – even vinyl.

It's also fun to think outside the box and be creative. Try turning something like paper (think vintage newspapers, brown paper bags, wrapping paper, etc.) or metal (such as an old baking tray) into your food photography backdrop. Pretty much anything is possible, but bear in mind backdrops that have a matt or near-matt finish will always make your star attraction look its very best. In addition, you're more likely to create show-stopping images if you use backdrops with lots of textures and details, because they add so much character and depth to your images. For this reason, I *never* iron my fabric backdrops. It's also why rustic wooden backdrops, or stone backdrops with different patterns and tones, make for such popular and enticing images. As always, in order to find what's right for you and your style, continuously check in with your heart's response and lean into what it reacts to most positively.

How backdrops affect light and shadow play

Your backdrop of choice will greatly impact the interplay between light and shadow in your image, because backdrops essentially function as absorbers or reflectors of light. For example, if you were to pick a dark wooden backdrop, you're more likely to create a moody image than if you were to select a white French linen tablecloth. That's because the dark wood will absorb more light and intensify your shadows; the white French linen will do the exact opposite. So interesting, right?!

But there's more! As I mentioned above, texture is *everything*, because the more texture you have, the more light and shadow points you get to play with! Every dent or bump on your backdrop will create tiny spots on which light particles can rest, as well as corners where shadows can get cosy and comfy. It is precisely this light and shadow play with your backdrop that will make your food photos look extra special.

Your backdrop is a stage

Essentially your backdrop is there to offer your star attraction a platform: a stage on which to shine. Consequently, when you choose your backdrop you need to carefully consider how it will enhance the features of your star attraction. Thinking through how the colour of your backdrop works with those of your star attraction is therefore fundamental see **Using colour with intention**, pages 55–68).

Just like a real stage, your backdrop will play a crucial role in evoking an emotion, setting the mood and helping you communicate your food story to your audience. As previously mentioned, it will do this through its light and shadow play as well as its injection (or lack) of colours and textures. So, please keep your food story, your colours, your star attraction and your light at the forefront of your mind as you select your backdrop. Remember, there's no right or wrong: just lots of opportunity to experiment, play and have fun.

NOTE You can download a mini guide with details on my top 5 favourite food photography backdrops and where to source them here: thelittleplantation.co.uk/food-photography-backdrops.

THE PERFECTLY
IMPERFECT BACKDROP IS:

MATT (or nearly matt)

full of **TEXTURES**, **PATTERNS** or **DETAILS**

an **ABSORBER** and/or **REFLECTOR** of light and shadow

THE RIGHT COLOUR for your chosen colour palette

a **KEY PLAYER** in your food story

A PLATFORM on which your star attraction can shine

part two

PLAYING

four

CREATIVE
COMPOSITION

creative composition

I considered calling this section 'The Rules of Composition'. But I hate rules and never follow them, so it seemed a bit hypocritical! For me, creativity isn't about rules: it's about having ideas and translating them into something beautiful. And that's exactly what I'd like to empower you to do through this section of the book – to turn the vision in your mind into a gorgeously composed image. The right composition can stop your audience from drifting through the frame and instead help draw their eyes straight to your star attraction, or enable them to flow through your image as you wish before settling right where you want them to.

It can be tricky to know how to compose an image, which is why I'm sharing some suggestions and ideas that past students of mine have found helpful when getting to grips with composition. As you move through the chapter, you notice that I don't refer to many commonly used composition techniques. This is not because I don't believe in them – they have their place, for sure – but because it's not how I approach my food photos (I told you I hate rules!). More importantly, my students have grasped some of the composition ideas I share below much more quickly than they have more technical composition concepts, which is why I've chosen this approach for you, too.

Compose first

Start by plating your food for a shot, arrange your bowls, plates and other props in the positions in which you want them to be.

Take a test shot or two as you're composing a scene to ensure that it translates well into an actual image. If the composition doesn't look right, move things around until they do. Only when you're 100 per cent happy with your composition should you start styling the food. If you style your food before you've perfected your composition, you risk losing precious time, during which your herbs can wilt, your ice cream can melt and your star attraction can lose its 'wow' factor. Starting with your composition will prepare you for the structure of a professional food photography shoot, so it's a good idea to make it a habit from the outset.

Negative space is a positive thing

Negative space gives your star attraction the opportunity to jump out of the frame, so it can be seen and fully appreciated. It also gives it space to breathe. Therefore, considering the negative space as much as the areas you fill is important in order to achieve a gorgeously composed food photo.

The balance between negative space and your food is most important when:

- you're aiming for a minimalistic look;

- you want to draw your audience's eye to your star attraction;

- you're creating shapes that need to stand out in order to guide the eye through your image.

How much is too much negative space? There's no such thing! It's really about *your* stylistic choice and the story you want to tell. So, as always, have a play and see what makes your heart sing.

composition to lead the eye

When you plan your composition, it is paramount that you think about how the eye will move through the frame and what you, as the creative, can do to allow that movement to be as pleasurable as possible. Over the years, I've found two things help tremendously in creating an organic flow through a food image. First, the concept of connecting the dots, and secondly, the idea of creating shapes.

Connecting the dots

It's easier to lead the eye through a food photo if the items (the 'dots') used in the shot are placed close enough together that you could connect them with an invisible line. This gives the eye direction and also enables the elements used to tell a bigger story together than they could on their own.

Creating shapes

Triangle, diamond, snake! I notice that when students come in for a workshop, they're often unsure about where to place their star attraction and all the supporting actors. And indeed, it can feel overwhelming. But every time I call out a shape in which to arrange the plates and props, they visibly relax.

Thinking about shapes when you compose an image gives you a starting point, an option you can play with and make your own. Shapes are there to help you plan how you want to guide your audience through the frame, and what you can do to ensure they notice your star attraction. Let's have a look at a couple of them, shall we?

TRIANGLES

The triangle is a simple, but very effective, composition tool, so it's a great way to see the power of composition work its magic. Just remember to keep the three elements that make up the triangle close enough together that you can easily connect them with an imaginary line.

LINES

Lines make for a bold and beautifully composed image. Add little extras or stray from the line a tiny bit to avoid making your image look overly stiff.

If you're using wooden planks as a backdrop or photographing the edge of your table, factor these additional lines into your composition and explore complementing them with round plates or softening them with clever prop placements.

SNAKE OR 'S' SHAPE

I *love* the flow of this composition technique, don't you?

THE WAYWARD CHILD

To ensure your shapes don't look too contrived, it's great having one or two elements step out of line. I call those elements 'wayward children', because they just won't conform to the order of the day thereby adding a dose of excitement to your frame.

DIAMOND

How can you be thoughtful and intentional about your composition, while at the same time making your image look effortless? You can create a relaxed, organic look by making your shapes perfectly imperfect. For example, you can make your scene look really natural by having one or two plates that are of a different size to the others, or by placing them in such a way that the shape, in this case a diamond, is a bit wonky.

NOTE **Bull's Eye:** When creating a diamond shape, please pay close attention to the area right in the centre of the frame, often referred to as the bull's eye. It's lovely to place a few props there, so that your audience's eye can easily and gently land on something beautiful.

A GENTLE CURVE

Can you see how the eye is gently led up towards the top left corner of the frame?

'L' SHAPE

I adore having items along two sides of my frame, especially when I'm shooting a flat lay (shooting from a bird's-eye view). That's because this way of composing an image creates lots of negative space while also giving you ample opportunity to tell your food story in detail.

'C' SHAPE

Another fabulous way to compose an image is by placing your items – be they plates, bowls or ingredients – at the edge of your frame in a 'C' shape. To still allow for the composition to have a natural sense of flow and not feel too staged or forced, use the principles of *wabi-sabi,* as outlined in **Perfect imperfection** (page 19). For example, you could have a few elements falling slightly outside the shape you've laid out, making it feel more dynamic and natural.

SYMMETRY

Composing an image using symmetry can be *so* fun. It's clearly staged, but symmetry with a hint of perfect imperfection makes for a really strong, bold composition statement.

THE FRAME

Using this as your composition technique is great if your star attraction is flying solo. All you need to do to make it work is place key ingredients or props around your star attraction to form a frame. The example shows how effective it can be as a composition tool.

LEVELS AND LAYERS

When you are shooting straight on or at an angle, it's nice to create visual points of interest at various heights. It keeps things intriguing and fun! Levels and layers can also come into play when you're shooting a flat lay.

Think about:

- what is in focus and what isn't;

- what is on the same level as the backdrop and what isn't;

- how many levels you are going to build into your composition.

The pink and green table cloths, the plates, the cake and then the flowers each introduce a new level and layer into the image.

THE SPIRAL

Taking its cue from nature, the spiral is dynamic and full of movement. It allows your eye to move through the entire frame before resting on the star attraction. This shape is so much fun to play with.

BREAKING YOUR SHAPES

Taking tiny components away can 'break' the shape you've created, while still keeping the framework of it there to guide your viewer's eye in the direction in which you want it to go. This is a bit mischievous and brings in an element of surprise. In addition, it makes your shape feel less forced and staged: win-win, right?

More to play with

MINIMALISM

Less can be more! Your star attraction can still look a million dollars even without a complex composition or lots of props.

Key to making this look work are:

- amazing **LIGHT** and **SHADOWS**

- creative use of your **APERTURE**

- a truly beautiful **STAR ATTRACTION**

- a good grasp of **COLOUR THEORY**

- a gorgeous **BACKDROP**

- ace **EDITING** skills

GOING OFF-CENTRE

If you like compositions where the focus is on your star attraction, you can make things more interesting by placing it off-centre. Doing so hints cheekily at the idea of perfect imperfection.

THE CASCADE

This composition technique works really well when photographing loose fruits and vegetables, although it can also be used when working with plated food. The idea is that you start with lots of food that then dwindles down to nearly nothing.

WORK THE CORNER

Having your supporting actors just barely creeping into the frame keeps viewers intrigued, without giving too much away. If you're unsure about how much to show and how much to cut off, shoot the whole scene, then crop down and play with framing it until it's just right.

RULE OF ODDS

Things always perk up when I use odd numbers: one cake, three bowls (another reason the triangle makes such a fantastic composition element), five spoons, etc. Although even numbers can work too (think symmetry), they can be trickier to get right. If you're feeling uninspired, or something's just not working, see if this simple approach will get you unstuck.

SCATTERED FOR EXTRA FUN

When you have multiples of the same foods, such as cookies, mini pavlovas, doughnuts or brownies, it can be really nice to arrange them very randomly and playfully. I usually try and show different sides, or break a piece off so that the viewer can get a good sense of the food in its entirety, but it's up to you.

IN THE MIDDLE

Placing your star attraction slap-bang in the middle of your shot is bold, beautiful and packs a real punch. If that's where you feel it deserves to be, go for it!

HUMAN TOUCH

When all else fails, bring in a hand model! No, seriously: hands can act as distraction points, as well as a way to draw your audience's eyes to where you want them to go. Hands can accentuate the shape you wish to create or simply breathe life into your frame. You can find lots of examples of this approach scattered throughout this book.

Stay creative, combine and play

What I love most about composition is that there's an infinite number of possibilities and endless ways to tell your story and express your creativity! What I've shared with you here are just a few ideas, something to get you fired up and raring to go. You can play around with *so* many more options; just remember to give your audience's eye direction and focus, and you simply can't go wrong.

share your work!

Want to share your compositions with me on Instagram? Please use the hashtag **#CREATIVEFOODPHOTOGRAPHY** when you post your image. I'd love to see your creations! Here are some of my favourite images with stunning compositions from my **#EATCAPTURESHARE** community (see credits on page 208).

five

STYLING
AND
PROPS

styling and props: food styling

One of the biggest challenges you face as a food photographer is that no one can actually eat your food. None of the people looking at your images can taste how flavourful your curry is, or experience how refreshing and delicious your home-made juice is. Therefore, you need to make sure that the visuals do all the talking for you, and allow your audience to imagine what it would be like to take a bite of one of your pancakes or lick the sorbet you've captured.

Food styling is the act of dressing up your star attraction for the camera and causing the audience to salivate and stare. Good food styling can translate your love and understanding of flavours and textures into a delectable food image that transmits perfectly how delicious life really is. Therefore, knowing how the eye and palette are connected, what flavours go together and how to finish off a dish with the perfect garnish makes all the difference.

Here you'll find some rough ideas and starting points to serve as inspiration and get your creative juices flowing. This list of food styling techniques is by no means exhaustive, but each one is effective and will work beautifully with whatever your individual style or food story is.

The bigger picture

ABUNDANCE

Although there are certainly exceptions, when it comes to food it's hard to argue against the idea that more is, well, more! One of the most inviting and visually attractive approaches to use in food styling is abundance, where your table of plenty looks like a feast fit for royalty. This is why it's always worth having a little extra food to hand to fill the scene and make your image an utter visual treat. In fact, having more ingredients than you technically need can also come in super handy when things don't go to plan, and you have to re-style and re-shoot a dish (see **When it all goes wrong**, page 200).

A BEAUTIFUL MESS

Want to make your food look beautiful, natural and effortless? Hoping to give your audience a sense that the food scene they're looking at just casually happened? We achieve this laid-back look, in part, by using the approach I call 'a beautiful mess'.

A beautiful mess is created when you take ingredients used to accompany or to make a dish to adorn the rest of your image, scattering them here and there. This method of food styling taps into the spirit of perfect imperfection. I'd recommend starting with a little bit at first and building the scene from there, adding more if and when required. Placing sprinkles of this and that near your main plate works beautifully. Take test shots as you go along and keep checking in with your heart to ensure you don't take it too far and create something chaotic instead of the beautiful mess you're aiming for.

GIVING YOUR FOOD SPACE TO BREATHE

What if you gravitate more towards minimalistic styling or simply don't enjoy filling up bowls to the rim? Consider using negative space on your plate instead, giving your star attraction the opportunity to 'breathe' and stand out. Having great props can help make this look work wonders (see **Props** on pages 165–177 for details).

COLOURS AND CONTRAST

Food styling is as much about understanding how colours work together as it is about arranging food. We've looked at combining colours in detail in **Using colour with intention** (pages 55–68), but suffice it to say here that using the right colours and contrast to create and dress your star attraction is fundamental to good food styling. In many ways, contrast adds interest and colours can do the styling for you.

So, you've overcooked the pasta, burned the toast, bruised the fruit and allowed your herbs to go yellow. If these foods are edible, please go ahead and eat them, but you'll need to reconsider making them your star attraction. It will make your photo shoot a whole lot easier if you start with gorgeous ingredients and perfectly cooked food. A star attraction that is in and of itself a beauty queen will ensure you're more likely to get the food image you're after. Consequently, carefully hand-select the ingredients you're going to use to ensure they are just right for the image you intend to create.

The delicious details

YIN AND YANG (AND THEN SOME)

Dividing your dish up into two (or more!) contrasting sections creates a visually striking look. It's a bold approach, but can work a treat and evoke a sense of thoughtful yet relaxed home cooking.

LAYERS

First of all, there's the literal approach to using layers in food styling: think layer cakes, parfaits, burgers and so on.

There's also the culinary approach to layering. In this scenario, layers aren't visible as such; they are present in terms of flavours, which the camera can magically pick up on, as each flavour is represented by a different ingredient. Incorporating a variety of flavourful ingredients into your food makes for some of the most visually stimulating and attention-grabbing styling on the planet.

Closely connected to layers and the flavour profile of a dish are textures. Different textures can make your star attraction not only more interesting to look at, but also a lot more fun to photograph. Let's explore this with a real-life example.

What's more boring than a plate of iceberg lettuce leaves with olive oil? Not much. Now visualise a plate full of warm, roasted carrots, crunchy nuts, fresh micro greens and a creamy dip. Much better, right? That's because all those different textures on which the mouth can feast, can be feasted on by the eye (and your camera) too. This is why we are often so drawn to food images with an abundance of textures, and why foods with lots of textured garnishes always look the bomb. Therefore, when you're developing the recipe you want to shoot, remember from the outset to include an exciting variety of complementary textures (and flavours).

HEIGHT

Your star attraction deserves to be seen! For this reason, remember to elevate your food. Rather than have key features disappear into the depths and shadows of deep bowls and pots, use grains, noodles and such to form a 'mattress' on which other ingredients can sit.

You can also stack your food (think pancake stacks or generously towering scoops of ice cream) for height, 'cos remember, the sky's the limit.

MOISTURE

Dried-out pasta, stews, fruits or herbs are never a good look, but it can easily happen if a shoot takes that little bit longer than hoped. Add a lovely dressing, a dash of olive oil or a creamy sauce to help liven up the dish. If nothing like that features in the recipe, grab a water spray instead: it can work wonders! The tiny little droplets it will leave on the food will flirt with the light and ensure your star attraction gets that gorgeous glow. Magic!

Movement

TORN, BITTEN, BROKEN AND CUT

These are clearly not official food styling terms, but I like them and use them all the time with my students! Tearing open a fruit, biting into a brownie, breaking off a piece of bread or cutting a slice of cake will all make your food scene feel more dynamic and alive. Whether you tear roughly or slice neatly is up to you. If you're after a relaxed, natural look and are shooting simpler, everyday foods, the imprecise act of tearing or biting might work better. However, if you wish your finished image to look quite formal, or if it includes a more elaborate dish such as a cheesecake, a neat slice can be the right way forward. As always, I invite you to consider the story you want to tell, then decide how to handle your food in the way that will tell it best.

SPIRAL

It doesn't get more dynamic than a spiral. This is a super-effective food styling trick and a lovely, easy way to finish off soups as well as breakfast bowls. Using a tiny spoon to drizzle over liquids such as cream or olive oil can help you be as precise as you need to be.

HALF-MOON CRESCENT

Like the spiral, the half-moon crescent is curvaceous and full of movement. It's great when decorating cakes and smoothie bowls and can provide a starting point when you're garnishing other foods, too. It's perhaps a more deliberate and obvious way of styling, but always effective.

Food styling may come to you naturally, especially if you have lots of experience in the kitchen, love developing recipes or are a pro at hosting dinner parties. Alternatively, food styling may end up being the part of the whole process you find trickiest. Either way, like everything mentioned in this book, play makes perfect. There is nothing more fun than playing with your food, so go for it and see what happens.

props

One day, when I was at the very beginning of my food photography journey and feeling rather dissatisfied with the shots I was capturing, I got a handful of food magazines, tore out all the food images I loved, placed them on my dining table and studied them intensely. I wanted to understand why my own images didn't look nearly as gorgeous as the ones lined up in front of me. I'd got to grips with my camera settings, I knew how to work the light, I could compose like no one's business, yet something was still missing. I just couldn't put my finger on it. But that day, as my frustration reached boiling point, the penny finally dropped.

A vintage knife, a linen napkin, that tiny little coffee cup in the corner that no one sees initially, and, of course, the plate on which your star attraction is served: these are just a few examples of that food photography essential, props. In fact, when I use the term 'props' here, I mean everything and anything that isn't your backdrop or the food you're shooting! Like supporting actors in a movie, you might not notice them at first glance, and you probably won't remember them afterwards, but they are *there*. They can bring that all-important final touch to your image and, without them, your star attraction simply can't shine so brightly. In other words, the right props can take your image from good to absolutely spectacular. Truth be told, it was once I had invested in a handful of beautiful props that things really started to take off for me.

In this section, we'll explore how to use props to tell your food story, how to curate the perfect collection to elevate your images, and how to make the most of their powerful impact.

Props to help you tell your story

Imagine you want to transport your audience to a traditional, rustic farmhouse kitchen in the middle of the English countryside. You've got a stunning vintage table as your backdrop and you've baked a gorgeous vegan apple crumble that's still piping hot. Candles adorn the scene, and all feels perfectly serene – until everyone's eyes drift towards the neon coloured plastic spoons and plates you're using to serve and eat the crumble. See how that one faux pas can totally ruin the story you're intending to tell?

Props complete the storyline and fill in the gaps of your narrative. They are there to enhance the mood you've set with your backdrop, colour and light choices, and to carry through the tone and feel you've planned for. Although they shouldn't take centre stage, they should support your star attraction and quietly communicate your food story to anyone who'll listen. This is why it is crucial to think carefully about which props will best serve your food story.

Props can include more than plates, glassware and cutlery, and thinking outside the box when it comes to your prop choices can add that personal touch to your food photo. For example, if you want to give your audience a sense that the strawberries in your image were freshly picked in the local woods, why not include a woven straw basket in your shot? Or are you setting out to take a still-life photo of the stunning herbs you've grown in your garden? Consider adding a vintage pair of scissors to your set-up. Recreating a busy breakfast scene? How about weaving a newspaper into your composition, alongside two cups of coffee? See where I'm going with this? Now it's your turn to consider how props can help tell *your* food story.

The power of props

PROPS PLAY WITH LIGHT AND SHADOW

The props you choose will have a huge impact on how light and shadow points dance across your food image. An obvious example would be a white plate, which will bounce back light, facilitating the creation of a lighter image, versus a dark plate, which will absorb light and assist in the shooting of a darker picture.

Props can play with light and shadow in more subtle ways, too. You could use cloths and fabrics to lift and brighten a slightly darker corner of an image, if required. Or, by placing (matt) silver spoons and forks on the table, you can provide small surfaces off which light particles can easily bounce, forming little sparkly points in your food photo.

Using shallow bowls rather than deep ones makes it easier for light particles to caress the food inside them and – as we'll discuss in a moment – using matt rather than shiny props will ensure nothing takes the spotlight away from your star attraction.

Good food photography is all about being thoughtful about light and shadow play. Bear this in mind when choosing your props: it will make a world of difference to your final capture.

PROPS TO ENHANCE YOUR COMPOSITION

As outlined in **Creative composition** (pages 131–151), props can be used to form shapes that guide the eye through the frame, but their presence can contribute towards a beautifully composed food image in many other ways, too. Outlined below is a list of fun ways to approach the use of props within the context of composition. It's by no means exhaustive, but hopefully will get your creative juices flowing.

PROPS CAN BE USED TO:

Fill negative spaces
in the frame.

Bring in an additional layer or texture for added
interest, depth and contrast.

Inject your image with
movement and colour.

Placing an object here guides the
eye towards the frame.

Accentuate the shape
you wish to create.

These blood oranges were so beautiful, a multitude of props simply wasn't necessary.

To prop or not to prop

There certainly are occasions where less is more and few or no props may be the ideal way forward. Ingredient shots are a great example of where stripping it down to the bare essentials can be super sexy; the lack of props can allow your audience to fully appreciate the beauty and intricacies of the food at hand.

Food photography for fine dining restaurants also relies on minimal props, or sometimes none at all. That's because the food styling they practise is so delicate and meticulously executed, it demands everyone's unwavering love and attention.

You might also find that using fewer props is simply what makes your heart beat fastest. Honour that and lean into this affinity, because it might just be your unique style stepping up to the mark.

For more ideas on how to nail a food image with few or no props at all, please revisit **Minimalism** page 146).

'...allow your audience to fully appreciate the *beauty* and *intricacies* of the food at hand.'

Curating your collection

Knowing how to choose and collect the right props is a skill that comes with time, developing as you establish your style and define your unique perspective. However, the prompts below should help pave the way for you to source props that are just right for you and your food story.

USE THE BEATING OF YOUR HEART AS A GUIDE!

Which are the props that you already own, or see in a flea market or on the pages of a cookbook, that make your heart skip a beat? Take note of them and analyse what they have in common in terms of style, colour, texture and shape. Doing so will help you get a better sense of your developing taste and what you naturally gravitate towards. If you can't yet find a common thread in the props you love, I'd encourage you to spend some time exploring all the options you fell in love with; forcing yourself to settle too early on one particular style is counterproductive. Just roll with it for as long as you need to, because the more options you try on, the likelier you are to settle on the one that truly fits you like a glove.

MATT WILL MAKE YOUR LIFE A WHOLE LOT EASIER

To avoid unsightly reflections, choose props that veer more towards matt rather than shiny.

TEXTURE ADDS DEPTH AND CHARACTER

Just like textured backdrops, plates and bowls with bumps and imperfections and cloths and napkins with creases or slightly frayed edges can add a thousand words to your food story. Alternatively, tiny details such as crooked rims on side plates or dainty hand-painted flowers on cups make wonderful additions to a scene. These little details set your props apart from their factory-made counterparts and will help set your image apart, too.

GOOD THINGS COME IN SMALL (AND SHALLOW) PACKAGES

Huge dinner plates are a nightmare to work with and can end up dominating the scene rather than guiding your audience's eye towards your star attraction. Deep bowls can make it hard to spot your food and sometimes even make it impossible for light particles to reach your star attraction. With that in mind, I suggest you use petite side plates, tiny pinch bowls, shallow pasta bowls and smaller-than-average cutlery. It will look fab, I promise!

NEUTRALS ARE NOT BORING!

Anything is possible, of course, and I'm not in a million years suggesting you can't reach for that ruby-red plate or the bowl with the large green polka dots, but food generally looks its very best when on a neutral-coloured plate that's not going to steal the limelight. There are always exceptions, and creativity knows no bounds, but neutrals are never boring when paired with gorgeously scrumptious foods.

BUT WHEN YOU DO USE COLOUR...

...refer to the colour wheel and/or use an overarching colour palette to guide your choices. Furthermore, think about the colours you love, the colours of the foods you tend to photograph most often and those of the backdrops at your disposal. Acquire props that complement that colour family, and you'll get the most use out of them.

THINK ABOUT HOW PIECES FIT TOGETHER

Before rushing out to purchase new props, carefully consider how they will work with what you've already got. Having different pieces that complement each other means you can mix and match to your heart's content. This will create a really organic, natural and relaxed food photo that feels thoughtful without looking too contrived.

ADDED EXTRAS

Make sure you begin by curating a solid props collection that consists of a handful of plates, bowls, glassware and cutlery. Once you have these essentials in place, make a list of items you're always wanting to incorporate into your set-ups but never have to hand. If you're a baker, this may include a vintage rolling pin; if you love shooting drinks, this may include some cool coasters. These are not die-hard essentials but can be great props to add on as you establish your style and delve deeper into the world of food photography.

REMEMBER THE FOOD STORY YOU WANT TO TELL

To return to the example we explored earlier, if you intend to recreate a rustic country kitchen, picking props that enhance this narrative is essential. When selecting props, refer back to your mood board and use the **Planning a Shoot** chapter (pages 35–99) to make sure you're on the right track.

a final note on props...

Propping likes and dislikes are as individual as favourite (vegan) ice cream flavours: there's no one size fits all, and that's a good thing. With this in mind, build your collection slowly, working with intention and direction, continuously referring back to what makes *your* heart beat faster. As long as you allow your props to showcase your style and tell your food story, you're bound to build a timeless collection that'll serve you for years to come.

'...build your collection slowly, working with *intention* and *direction*, continuously referring back to what makes *your* heart beat faster'.

case studies

Kolamba

BRIEF

Create images that honour traditional foods and flavours from Sri Lanka, while communicating the restaurant's elegant yet modern, fresh yet rustic approach. Photograph food the way it would be served in the restaurant.

BEHIND THE SHOTS

Gotu kola is a traditional herb eaten abundantly in Sri Lanka, yet largely unknown to Kolamba's UK-based audience. Hence, the client wanted to show what gotu kola looks like raw as well as how it's served in the restaurant. We agreed on a cooler colour palette and minimal styling to allow the herb to take centre stage.

This refreshing **ice coffee** is served simply in the restaurant, without any garnishing or unnecessary extras. Consequently, to keep the set up interesting, we introduced action into the image, as well as the owner's hands.

When shooting **curries** like the one you see here, I find it really important to move away from the narrative that traditional foods from Asia, the Caribbean or Africa are somehow not attractive, that they are 'less than' or hard to photograph. Instead, I focus on the food's own unique beauty and drool factor. In the case of this delicious curry, that included its vibrant colour and lush, moist mouth feel, which I emphasised at the editing stage by increasing the yellow saturation and luminance.

Tofuture

BRIEF

Capture vegan tofu-based recipes that look delicious, yet achievable! The client left the visuals of the brief very open, which meant lots of creative freedom – as well as ample opportunity to get the imagery wrong!

BEHIND THE SHOTS

When I work with clients who are excited about lots of different food photography styles, I often provide two to three different options, usually including a more toned-down look, as well as one using bolder colours (as you can see in the two vegan cheesecake images below).

When shooting foods that are visually less impactful, like this vegan **tofu Christmas loaf**, I often recommend shooting the food with accompaniments, in order to bring in more colours and textures. Here, for example, the puree, Brussels sprouts and ground pepper add some much-needed texture, colour and contrast.

Casseroles can be a joy to eat, but require extra TLC, both when styling and when shooting! While preparing the dish, we used the back of a spoon to introduce patterns into the mashed potato topping, which we further accentuated with a blow torch! When it was time to photograph the casserole, we shot it untouched first before breaking the dish down and taking numerous shots along the way.

La Boulangère - Vegan range

BRIEF

Photograph the company's new vegan range, alluding to its traditional French origins and farmhouse kitchen style as well as the product's plant-based credentials. Including one or both of the brand's colours (red and/or yellow) would be a bonus.

BEHIND THE SHOT

The **vegan pains au chocolat** (and chocolate sauce) needed to be warm so that the chocolate would ooze out, yet the ice cream needed to be cold enough to hold its shape. To make the shot happen, we created the ice cream scoops and then returned them to the freezer while we warmed up the pastry and set up the scene. Then, at the final moment, we took the ice cream out of the freezer before drizzling over the hot chocolate sauce. Done!

As you know, I believe that adding texture and moisture is everything in food styling, but what if the product needs to be shot without any added extras? That's what the client asked for when it came to their **vegan croissants**.

To give the shot a sense of movement and interest, the croissant was cut into pieces, with crumbs scattered here and there. Plants were included to hint at its plant-based ingredients and the yellow scarf (which was actually a T-shirt) allowed for one of the client's brand colours to form part of the scene, too.

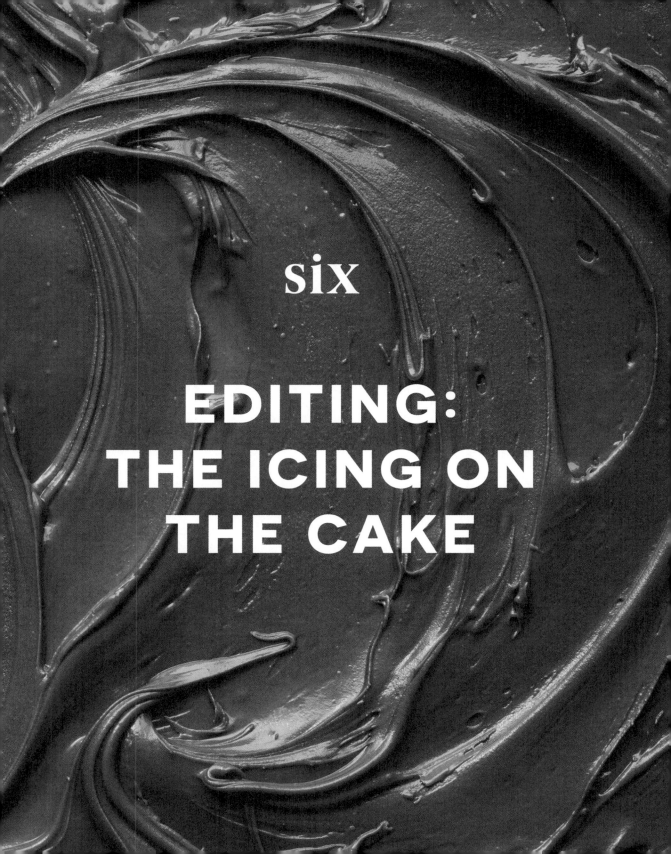

six

EDITING: THE ICING ON THE CAKE

editing: the icing on the cake

At the start of this book, I promised you that I wouldn't provide you with linear answers, and that you wouldn't be presented with a cookie-cutter approach to food photography anywhere on these pages. I'm committed to keeping this promise until the very end, which means you won't find boring one-size-fits-all instructions to editing your food photos in this book either. In all honesty, there aren't any, and suggesting otherwise would be misleading.

This section is less about the basic technicalities of editing and more about how to use it to create your signature food photography look, the benefits of which we've explored in so much depth already. (If you *are* looking for a technical step-by-step outline on editing, may I suggest you consider joining my online food photography and food styling course, where I talk you through the process of editing from start to finish).

Just like the photography process, the editing process offers endless possibilities, not only to fine-tune your image, but also to give it your unique touch. That can feel terribly overwhelming if you aren't quite sure what you want to achieve through editing, but it can be super invigorating if you know exactly what mood you're after and what food story you want to tell.

EDITED

UNEDITED

EDITED

UNEDITED

the joy of a clear vision

To make editing as joyful an experience as possible, it's immensely helpful to go into it with an end goal in mind, a specific finish you're striving for. As you sit down to work through your images in post-processing, ask yourself the questions below to ensure you nail the look you're after.

WHO AM I CREATING FOR?

If you're creating for a client, take a look at the images on their website, menu, etc. Do they have a particular feel, and how can you ensure through your editing that your shots will comfortably sit alongside their existing images? Did the client provide you with a mood board and, if so, does it give any hints as to the editing style they are looking for?

If you're creating for yourself, as always, use your heart's response as your guide through the editing maze.

WHAT STORY AM I TELLING?

What mood are you trying to evoke, and what scene have you created? Use editing to continue telling your food story in the best way possible. If you're telling a story with a dark and cosy mood, you might try introducing a vignette and deepening your shadows. If you're telling the story about the freshness of spring produce, you might try upping your vibrance and being playful with your colours. There are endless possibilities, so it's important to keep referring back to your mood board and reminding yourself of your intention.

This shot is all about the pour, which means I used the brush tool to further emphasise the central glass, the juice and the bottle.

EDITED   **UNEDITED**

IS YOUR STAR SHINING?

What can you do through your editing choices to further ensure all eyes are on the star attraction? This may include using a vignette to cleverly lead the eye to a particular point in the frame. It might mean making use of the adjustment brush or radial filter, thereby giving your star attraction some extra-special editing treatment. It could also involve manipulating the colours of your star attraction on your HSL (Hue, Saturation and Luminance) so they jump off the page. You're the artist, so you get to decide what goes.

WHAT COLOUR PALETTE AM I WORKING WITH?

What are the important, dominant colours in your image? Can you work with your panel to fine-tune them? Looking at some of the features on your basics panel, including temperature, blacks, whites and saturation, will further allow you to manipulate how your colours look and ensure you get them just right.

WHAT'S MY LIGHT AND SHADOW PLAY?

Often students will shoot an image with a clear and specific light and shadow interplay in mind, only to edit it all out! Instead, remind yourself of how you shot your image in the first place, remembering the light and shadows you naturally captured and chose to shoot. Work with features on your basics panel, such as exposure, highlights, shadows, whites and blacks, to accentuate what you've already captured so beautifully with your camera!

EDITED **UNEDITED**

To make this brighter shot feel cosy and a touch moody, the shadows were deepened during the editing process.

Presets for the win

Presets (sometimes also referred to as filters) allow you to save your editing settings and apply them on countless images. Presets also enable you to pull all your photos together so they have a similar, consistent look – *your* look – and can sit together beautifully on your website, in a cookbook or on any of the social media platforms where you share your work.

Presets save you a lot of editing time and are great if you notice that you're consistently editing in a very similar manner. If you're still searching for your style, though, perhaps give them a miss until you're clearer about the look you're after, or have a handful of different presets you can play with until you've found the right one(s).

UNEDITED

PRESET 1

PRESET 2

PRESET 3

UNEDITED

EDITED

a final thought on editing...

Editing is the icing on the cake, the final touch that brings all your planning and hard work to a beautiful finish. As with everything outlined in this book, give yourself time to explore your options until you find what resonates with you and allows you to create a look you're truly happy with.

'Editing is the icing on the cake, the *final touch* that brings all your planning and hard work to a beautiful finish.'

seven

PLAY MAKES PERFECT

play makes perfect

My food photography workshops may be officially called 'workshops' on my website, but in my mind I actually refer to them as 'playtime'. I use the term *play*time because it instantly and visibly puts my students at ease, evoking memories of childhood and boundless joy. *Play*time (compared to *work*shop) also gives us permission to be inquisitive, mischievous, bold and imaginative: to do things that are not normally allowed in your day-to-day life.

Playtime paves the way for fun and discovery as well as lots of self-reflection. That's because, when you surrender to creative play in your food photography and styling, you aren't attached to the outcome. Instead, you're there to enjoy the process. Use every moment of your playtime as a chance to try new things and liberally explore what makes your heart beat faster. It's kind of like when you used to build sandcastles on the beach as a child. Sure, it felt amazing when it all came together and you created a beautiful sandcastle, but it was also so much fun (and so fabulous!) when the waves washed away the fruits of your labour and you had to do it all again. Do you know what I mean?

when it all goes wrong

I'm ashamed to say I've cried over food photography shoots gone wrong. And not just tiny tears; oh no, full-blown temper tantrums. In other words, I know what it's like to pour your heart and soul into an image, only to find that it simply doesn't come together, no matter how hard you try.

Through creative play, practice and experience, those situations are a rarity now. When things *do* go pear-shaped, I ask myself the questions we outline on page 203 and revisit my mood board. More often than not, this helps me turn what looks like a dog's dinner into a delectable dish and capture the shot I'm after.

But there are still days where my star attraction falls apart before my eyes, those light particles simply won't shine brightly or the supporting actors, whether they are plates, cloths or cutlery, go on strike. Time-permitting, I abandon ship, take note of what didn't work, refine my mood board and try again another day, aiming to return to it when things have calmed down and I feel refreshed, energised and creatively replenished. If this isn't a possibility and the photograph absolutely has to be taken right there and then, I set out to pinpoint exactly why the image isn't working. Armed with this new-found information, I start all over again.

If things go wrong and you find yourself in a place where you have to leave it and attempt it again another time, I invite you to try and cultivate a new mindset to bring along to your reshoot. Rather than doubt yourself and linger on all the negative emotions, look at a failed shoot as a gift and an incredible learning opportunity. From personal experience, I can promise that this act of turning the narrative of a failed shoot on its head can work wonders.

The process of finding inspiration helps you uncover what you like; the process of failure helps you uncover what you don't like. Both are of equal value and important stepping stones on your journey to becoming the food photographer you're destined to be. Play makes perfect, remember – and having to do it all over again just means another chance to play.

evaluating your work

So, if a shoot doesn't reduce you to tears or have you jumping for joy, how do you know if what you're creating is good enough? More often than not, you're probably your own worst critic: the stereotypical artist who is never satisfied with their work. Sound familiar? To some degree, a level of restlessness is necessary to continuously push yourself forward and strive for more. However, appreciating the images you've shot in the here and now, and distinguishing between what's actually pretty drool-worthy and what needs some serious fine-tuning is an important skill to have.

Because food photography is art, and art is subjective, there's never a clear-cut 'good' or 'bad'. What is clear-cut, though, is your heart's response. This is why continuously tuning into what makes it beat faster throughout your food photography shoot is paramount. It's why I recommend you take a number of test shots as you're composing your scene (see **Creative Composition**, pages 131–151) and styling your star attraction, all the while checking in with yourself to ensure you're happy with the way things are going. If you are, awesome! If you're not, please don't throw the baby out with the bath water. Instead stop, take stock and analyse where you've gone astray and what needs adjusting and changing.

Asking yourself the following questions might help you
discover what's not working:

LIGHT

Is your star attraction shining brightly, and are your camera settings enhancing
light and shadow play to its advantage?

COMPOSITION

Are you guiding your audience's eye through the frame and ensuring it lands
exact where you want it to?

STYLING

Is your star attraction dressed to impress, and are all the supporting actors
(aka your props) making it look a million dollars?

ANGLES

Is this angle flattering, or is it causing your star attraction's perfect
imperfections to look downright ugly?

In my experience, things usually perk up when these points are addressed.
If not, I invite you to revisit your mood board once more to see where else
things need to be reshuffled.

something small to make you smile...

The more you play at food photography and styling, the better you get. In other words, play makes perfect. Creating something for your eyes only and going through the whole process for the sheer pleasure of styling and shooting your star attraction, just because you can, is an empowering, liberating experience! I invite you to keep playing, to keep exploring. I promise that it *will* make you a better food photographer, and help you create those stand-out images that really make your heart sing.

ABOUT THE AUTHOR

Kimberly Espinel is an award-winning food photographer, stylist, blogger and educator, having taught thousands of students from around the world the art of food photography and styling. She's known for her warm and generous teaching style, as well as her bold use of colours and love of plant-based foods. Kimberly is the host of the *Eat Capture Share* podcast and the creator of the incredibly popular Instagram food photography challenge #eatcaptureshare, which has had more than 100,000 entries from around the world – and counting!

Kimberly runs sold-out online and in-person one-to-one and group food photography and food styling workshops. She can be found at thelittleplantation.co.uk as well as **@thelittleplantation** and **@eatcaptureshare_** on Instagram.

thank you

To the man and the boy in my life, Santiago and Gabriel: you are the two best things that have ever happened to me, and your incredible support and endless patience allowed this book to come to life. I love you both SO much!

To Christina and Beatriz, TLP HQ would be nothing without you. Thank you for helping me build my creative business. Without your hard work and non-stop cheerleading, none of this would be possible.

To my A-Team: Fiona Humberstone, I could not have asked for a better art director; your energy and creative vision helped push this project to completion. Elizabeth Cairn, officially the most supportive structural editor on the planet: I honestly don´t know how you turned our simple conversation in a cafe into the outline of this book! Emily Voller, you got me and my style instantly and brought my hopes and dreams for this book to life with your gorgeous design. Tara O´Sullivan, you´re such a sweet line editor, super grateful no one got to see my typos and grammatical errors but you.

To my parents: I owe it all to you

To Sumera and Josh: how you put up with me talking about this book for months, I do not know, but our rich conversations helped make this book what it is today.

To everyone who contributed their work to this book: thank you from the bottom of my heart.

To the #eatcaptureshare community: your curiosity and creativity helped inform the direction of this book. I am in awe of all the gorgeous work you share with the world and I'm honoured to be able to go on this photography journey with you.

To my food photography students: thank you for making me a better teacher, for helping me understand what I need to explain more thoroughly and for showing me how to empower you to be the awesome food photographers and stylists I know you can be. I am eternally grateful to have been able to serve you on your creative path.

Creative Food Photography is jam packed with useful tips and guidance for finding your own unique style of visual story telling. If you're looking to deepen your knowledge or are just beginning your food photography journey—this book is a great place to start.

AMY CHAPLIN James Beard award-winning author of *Whole Food Cooking Every Day* and *At Home in the Whole Food Kitchen*

An exceptionally talented stylist and photographer, Kimberly's warm and generous teaching style offers everybody a place at the table to share in her magic. She's also an all-round excellent human, a quality you see shining through in everything she creates – from her food, to her images, to this beautiful book.

SARA TASKER author of *Hashtag Authentic*, Instagram expert and photographer at Me and Orla

Kimberly's presence in the world of food photography and styling is a gift. She has the amazing ability to express her own distinct style in her work while simultaneously teaching others how to cultivate their own unique visual voice through her educational offerings.

JOANIE SIMON Food photographer at The Bite Shot

Kimberly's food photography is stunning and I can't think of a better person to write a book about food photography and styling. If you love beautiful images of food, you'll love this book.

DR MEGAN ROSSI author of *Eat Yourself Healthy*, gut expert at *The Gut Health Doctor*

What I love about what Kimberly does is that she is willing to share her innate sense for food styling and photography – many people with her talent wouldn't strive to make it accessible for others. But Kimberly truly wants everyone to be able to make beautiful, authentic content and share it, too, which is a rare and special thing.

REBECCA SEAL author and *Sunday Brunch* presenter

Kimberly is one of the most generous, inspiring photographers and educators that I've had the pleasure of teaching with on several occasions. She engages with students in a relatable way, imparting so much knowledge and experience, and I have no doubt that this book is going to be a game-changer for food photographers at all stages of their career.

LAUREN CARIS SHORT Food photographer and educator, Food Photography Academy

While some food photography teachers focus on achieving one particular style, Kimberly encourages her students to find their unique visual voices through exercises in colour, lighting and composition. Her beautiful images and photography challenges never fail to inspire me!

ALANNA TAYLOR-TOBIN author and photographer of *Alternative Baker* and The Bojon Gourmet blog

Published by Delish Books

DELISH BOOKS

First published in Great Britain 2021.

TEXT © Kimberly Espinel, 2021.

ISBN: 978-1-5272-5835-8

1 2 3 4 5 6 7 8 9

LINE EDITOR: Tara O'Sullivan
STRUCTURE EDITOR: Elizabeth Cairns
ART DIRECTION: Fiona Humberstone
TYPE-SETTING AND DESIGN: Emily Voller

Printed and bound in Latvia.

PHOTOGRAPHY AND STYLING © Kimberly Espinel.

Apart from the following

PHOTOGRAPHY
Jo Szymkiewicz (6)
Dominika Durianova (117, left)

PHOTOGRAPHY AND STYLING:
Felicia Chuo @fliske (151, top left)
Viola Minerva Virtamo @violaminerva (151, top centre)
Pratiba Bhat @pratibabhat (151, top right)
Erica Ferraroni @ferraronierica (151, centre left)
Shiela Cruz @flavourfilled (151, centre)
Jella Bertell @vaimomatskuu (151, centre right)
Ritumbhara Chinnabalan @happytummybyritumbhara (151, bottom left)
Christall Lowe @christall.lowe (151, bottom centre)
Stefania Gambella @stefiinstax (151, bottom right)

STYLING:
Kimberly Espinel, Leiliane Valadares, Viola Hou (cover)
Kimberly Espinel, Silvia Bifaro (44; 45; 62; 67, right; 84, right)
Kimberly Espinel, Leiliane Valadares (60; 115; 169, top right; 181; 186; 188, top left; 188, top right; 201)
Kimberly Espinel, Beatriz Moreno (83, right; 85, left; 99)
Kimberly Espinel, Aimee Twigger (96; 135; 137, right)
Kimberly Espinel, C.R. Tan (97)
Kimberly Espinel, Lauren Caris (141; 142, left)
Kimberly Espinel, Nisha Weerasekera (160, left; 178, 179)
Natalie Penny, (117, right; 128)
Barbora Baretic (102)